The Purpose and Power of Mentorship

Compiled by

***Dr. Amanda H. Goodson
& Marvin Carolina Jr.***

The Purpose and Power of Mentorship
Compiled by Dr. Amanda H. Goodson and Marvin Carolina Jr.
Featured authors (in alphabetical order): Valeene Bedford, Marvin Carolina Jr., Vernette Elliott, Dr. Amanda H. Goodson, Lonnie Goodson, P. Leon King, Rosalind Longmire, Terri Luna, Jeannie Lynch, Robert W. Merriweather, Dr. Lamata Mitchell, Daniel Scott, Odetta Scott, Dwayne Simpson, Laura Tremaine, Dr. Karockas Watkins

© 2020 by Amanda H. Goodson and Marvin Carolina Jr.
All rights reserved.

Editing: Adam Colwell's WriteWorks, LLC, Adam Colwell and Ginger Colwell
Book Design: Inktobook.com
Published by Amanda Goodson Global, LLC

Printed in the United States of America
ISBN (Paperback): 978-1-951501-09-9
ISBN (eBook): 978-1-951501-11-2

Scripture taken from THE HOLY BIBLE, NEW INTERNATIONAL VERSION ®. Copyright©
1973, 1978, 1984, 2011 by Biblica, Inc.™. Used by permission of Zondervan

All rights reserved. Except in the case of brief quotations embodied in critical articles and reviews, no portion of this book may be reproduced, stored in a retrieval system, or transmitted in any form or by any means—electronic, mechanical, photocopy, recording, scanning, or other—without the prior written permission from the author. None of the material in this book may be reproduced for any commercial promotion, advertising or sale of a product or service.

A Note from the Authors

We are saddened about the current situation in the United States. The impact of the COVID-19 pandemic and the social unrest stemming from systemic racism has deeply wounded our nation and its people. We believe it will be through active and genuine leadership and mentorship that we can get to a renewed place of peace and wholeness as a country and as Americans.

June 2020

Acknowledgments

WE ARE GRATEFUL for how Jesus brought together such a extraordinary group of individuals to share their incredible insights.

Dwayne Simpson

I want to thank my wife, Debra, daughter, Natalie, and grandsons, Isaiah and Kyson, for their patience and support throughout my career and in the writing of this book.

Valeene Bedford

In loving memory of my parents, John and Effie Gregory, who taught me by example that it is a greater blessing to give than to receive. My heartfelt appreciation, also, to my supportive spouse, Carl Bedford, my life coaches, and those who honored me in their encouragement to be a part of this project.

Daniel Scott

I am honored to be part of this wonderful group of co-authors and am blessed to be have been asked to support this amazing project. Special thanks to my family, friends, and mentors who continue to inspire me to live my purpose.

Laura Tremaine

To my wonderful husband, Jerry Schuster, who has brought more joy to my life than I ever dreamed possible. Every moment together is so precious to me and each day a gift. You were so worth the long wait.

Lonnie Goodson

I'd like to acknowledge my lovely wife for everything that she does to make all things work well for me and my family. To my son, Jelonni, I acknowledge you, and I am very proud of you. Also, I am delighted to acknowledge so many mentors, coaches, and sponsors who helped me to be successful on my continued journey. To my family, my sister, and my brother, know that I love you, and I appreciate all that you do for me.

Terri Luna

I thank God for every gift and talent He blessed me to have and to share. I am grateful for the love-filled parenting of Janice and Emanuel Luna. Their guidance allowed me to believe I could accomplish anything and that any success I experienced was to be shared with those in need. Finally, I cherish the love, support, and encouragement I always find in my sister and best friend, Merrie Smith. I am because they are.

Rosalind Longmire

Thank you to all who assisted me through this incredible endeavor. Special thanks to my family and friends for all of your love and support during this venture. Finally, to all my mentors, coaches, and sponsor, I am truly grateful for the encouragement and opportunities that contributed to my accomplishments on my journey to purpose.

Marvin Carolina Jr.

I would like to acknowledge and thank my parents, Marvin Sr. and Jeannette Carolina. They were my first mentors, guiding, protecting, and allowing my imagination and dreams to meet reality. I also want to thank all of my coaches, teachers, mentors, friends, and colleagues that poured into me all of the wonderful results that are going out today. Finally, I want to thank my wife, Michelle, who continues to support and encourage me every day. "What goes in the well will come up in the bucket." Thanks for putting great things in the well.

Dr. Amanda H. Goodson

I'd like to thank my family for their continued support in my endeavors to write, speak, train, and coach, along with so many other things that I have the opportunity to be blessed to do. My husband, Lonnie: you are such an amazing man and you are perfect for me. To my son, Jelonni, thank you for loving me how I am and allowing me to love you back. To my mom, sister, and extended family, thank you so very much for always being there for me. Je're, thank you for your tireless support to everything I do.

Robert W. Merriweather

I express sincere gratitude to the individuals who inspired, challenged, and celebrated me through their dedication of time to my maturation as a successful leader. In addition, thank you to those that made this work a reality. And, most importantly, to God and family who are the delight, infrastructure, and solace to my being.

Dr. Lamata Mitchell

I would like to acknowledge my faithful husband, Kent, who continues to be my rock and continuous supporter. Also, to my wonderful children and special friends, thank you for always being there. I appreciate all my colleagues and significantly special people who made a difference for me by encouraging and exhorting me along the way. With heartfelt thanks, I smile as I acknowledge Jamella Gory and Dr. Amanda H. Goodson for being convinced that I had something to say as a leader and mentor. I am grateful to God for His kindness and for all of you.

Dr. Karockas Watkins

I would like to acknowledge my lovely wife, Audra, who stood by my side and encouraged me with this project. Also, to my family and special friends, thank you for the encouragement and support. I appreciate all the business and spiritual mentors and exceptional people who made a difference for me by seeing something special and great inside of me. I am in this place in life because of others giving of themselves into me. I am grateful to God for His grace and for you all.

Odetta Scott

A sincere thank you to my husband, parents, family, and friends. Having you in my corner to provide support has proved invaluable. Thank you to all my mentors who have poured into me, and to my mentees who have allowed me to pour into them. Each one reach one!

P. Leon King

I would like to acknowledge my lovely wife, Sharon, who stood by my side and encouraged me every step of the way. Also, to my family and special friends, thank you for the encouragement and support. I appreciate all the mentors and exceptional people who made a difference for me by seeing something special great inside of me. I am grateful to God for His grace and for all of you.

Jeannie Lynch

I would love to praise my God, with whom all things are possible. A special thank you to all the women I have mentored both in business and in their spiritual walks. Thank you for teaching me. Thank you for allowing me into your beautiful stories. Thank you for trusting me enough to share. Thank you to all the wise women who have mentored me and taught me the many qualities that are required to be a good mentor. I am eternally grateful.

Vernette Elliott

To my wonderful husband, friend, and encourager, Anthony Elliott, who made this possible. You helped me to see the vision and provided me with the strength and encouragement to keep going. You are a great man of God and faith. Thank you. To my daughters, Davina and Simone, thank you for your continued love and support.

Table of Contents

FLOW WITH THE PURPOSE—UNLEASH THE POWER! ... xiii

CHAPTER ONE ... 1
All Things Happen for a Reason – Dwayne Simpson

CHAPTER TWO ... 11
The Thriving of Mankind – Valeene Bedford

CHAPTER THREE ... 25
Rite of Passage – Daniel Scott

CHAPTER FOUR ... 35
An Invaluable Collaboration – Laura Tremaine

CHAPTER FIVE ... 45
Stages and Phases – Lonnie Goodson

CHAPTER SIX ... 53
Finding the Freedom – Terri Luna

CHAPTER SEVEN ... 65
Come Into Your Own – Rosalind Longmire

CHAPTER EIGHT 73
Moments of Impact – Marvin Carolina Jr.

CHAPTER NINE 83
Give Back: Dr. Amanda H. Goodson

CHAPTER TEN 93
Get in the Right Lane – Robert W. Merriweather

CHAPTER ELEVEN 103
A Legacy of Giving Back – Dr. Lamata Mitchell

CHAPTER TWELVE 117
Blessed to be a Blessing – Dr. Karockas Watkins

CHAPTER THIRTEEN 127
Full Circle – Odetta Scott

CHAPTER FOURTEEN 137
Profound Effect – P. Leon King

CHAPTER FIFTEEN 145
The Best Version – Jeannie Lynch

CHAPTER SIXTEEN 153
Trust and Confidence – Vernette Elliott

Flow with the Purpose—Unleash the Power!

men-tor-ship (*noun*)

The transfer of knowledge, experience, and skill from one person to another person, team, or organization that moves them forward in a positive way.

THAT'S THE SIMPLE yet profound definition of mentorship—yet it is really so much more than that.

And it's never been more *needed* than now.

As 2020 got underway, we had received more requests for mentorship over the previous year than ever before. It seems more and more people—particularly Millennials receiving from Baby Boomers—are desiring mentorship for themselves, or even to learn how to become a mentor to others.

We get it! After all, we've mentored each other for years. We know the adage from the book of Proverbs in the Bible about "iron sharpening iron" is so true. Some would consider us to be at the pinnacle of our careers, yet we not only

actively mentor others, but we are also being mentored. We know there is still so much to learn, and we enthusiastically engage in the mentoring process because we know the value it brings for both the mentor and the mentee.
That's why we have created this book.

The Purpose and Power of Mentorship will introduce you to 16 fabulous and gifted individuals who have given and received mentorship and realized the incredible difference it has made in their lives as well as the lives of others.

Dwayne Simpson has discovered that the biggest barriers to success that exist in people's minds are themselves and the fear of failure. He encourages you to push through, get back up, and start doing what you need to do to make a significant impact.

Valeene Bedford shares her belief that mentoring itself is based on the propagation and thriving of mankind, and she reveals The Mentoring Program she has created for disadvantaged high school youth in her community.

Daniel Scott tells us about the mentorship by example model that he discovered from his parents and extended family using a most unusual method. He will teach you how a fruitful life is one spent in service of others.

Laura Tremaine unveils how mentorship has increased her awareness of her role in society and her responsibility to help others and improve our world while striving to serve as a positive catalyst for kindness.

Lonnie Goodson looks at his belief that every stage of life requires mentorship. Whether it comes from parents, siblings, relatives, pastors, teachers, or supervisors, things change, and you have to be adaptable.

Terri Luna tells of living for the "aha" moment when her clients discover they have the answer to the opportunity they brought to her as a leadership and performance coach. She looks deeper at the purpose and joy found in mentoring and coaching.

Rosalind Longmire shares how the mentors who came into her life along the way also equipped her to be an effective mentor by nurturing, guiding, and being a role model to others. She says that it's the little things you do to pour into people that are the greatest things you can possibly do for others.

Marvin Carolina Jr. shares how mentorship begins in our lives as we observe people, and that the three basic aspects to helping people as he mentors others are trust, respect, and best interest.

Dr. Amanda H. Goodson establishes the importance of mentorship in advocating a "Seven Up," referring to the number of mentors or coaches anyone should have at any one time. She also introduces how a mentor is a futurist—someone who helps you think 10 or even 20 years ahead of where you are now.

Robert W. Merriweather talks about his "Get in the Right Lane" process that focuses on the three areas of coaching, mentoring, and sponsoring. He declares why the saying, "Say what you mean, and mean what you say," is a principle he's learned to value as he's worked with others.

Dr. Lamata Mitchell discusses why she believes the community college is a powerful tool for transforming lives, and how it is her purpose to ensure the educators and students she serves now and in the future have been able to experience the vast benefits of mentorship.

Dr. Karockas Watkins looks at the power of mentorship (people helping you get to your destiny) and the power of mentors: individuals who support you and speak into you so that you can be positioned to succeed by fulfilling that destiny.

Odetta Scott tells how her mentoring experiences have shown her that it still goes back to her life motto of "each one reach one" as we look for opportunities to position ourselves and others to navigate to their destiny. We just have to help each other.

P. Leon King talks about some of his most significant mentoring experiences from different times in his life. He reminds you that people see you every day—and your example has an effect on them that is profound.

Jeannie Lynch reveals how the difference between mediocrity and greatness is caring for one another and loving each other. She describes her goal as a mentor to assist people in being the best version of themselves.

Vernette Elliott shares how she discovered that mentoring is not about her. It is all about helping somebody else, even those you might not like. Her story will reveal mentoring as a priceless experience that will enhance your learning and development in all walks of life.

The *purpose* of mentorship flows from its process. Think of it as laying the foundation of a building. The process, which is carried out continuously in varying ways by different

Flow with the Purpose—Unleash the Power!

mentors, forms the solid foundational pieces that can then be used to put up the walls, set up the roof, and complete the structure. That's where the *power* of mentorship comes through. From that structure, creative tension is produced that is tangible, relevant, and relatable. This fosters a relationship and a level of trust so that the mentor can really speak to the problem or challenge and leverage it, unleashing power that is much like pressing on the accelerator of a finely tuned sports car. It speeds you forward and provides the fuel of excellence that will get you from one place to the next, revealing the potential that you may have never otherwise seen in yourself.

The purpose and power of mentorship makes you the architect of *who you are* as a professional and as a person. It gives you lift wherever you are in your career or in the community, providing a competitive advantage and an edge in situational leadership. It teaches you to understand your most important values, helps with your personal presence and brand, and equips you to be resistant and responsible because you have a strategy and the ability to inspire yourself to action. It also positions you to see how coaching (which is also covered often in this book) can supplement your mentorship experience, and what sponsorship is and how such advocacy is vital.

The Purpose and Power of Mentorship is relevant and relatable for those in business and industry, in academia, and in non-profit organizations, as well as those involved in the local community. As you read, it is our sincere hope that you will desire to become mentored, as well as see what you can offer as a mentor to others.

You have information sitting on your mental shelf. Some you are using, and some you are not. But you can help

THE PURPOSE AND POWER OF MENTORSHIP

somebody else out with it while enjoying the benefit of better organizing your thoughts as you start to understand and share the knowledge, experience, and skill you possess. So, join us—and discover the purpose and power for yourself!

Dr. Amanda H. Goodson
Marvin Carolina Jr.

The next anthology book from Amanda Goodson Global on *The ABC's of Influence* is scheduled for release in early 2021.

1

All Things Happen for a Reason

Dwayne Simpson

HAVING WORKED FOR several major aerospace and defense companies over the past 37 years, I have been in more professional development programs than the average Joe. I probably understand the ins and outs of most of them and what I would consider to be the pros and cons of each one. Throughout my career, I have also mentored, coached, and developed a lot of people, many of whom are now in senior leadership roles, and I have built a positive network that I now use at DND Global Enterprises, my new company, to fully execute my skills in recruiting, screening, hiring, developing, coaching, and helping people get positions.

Yet it wasn't until just two years ago that I had my first coach—and my experience with her continues to resonate with me to this day as I enter the last quarter of my career and strive to set myself up for when I quit working full-time.

Her name is Dawn Owens, and she is author of the book, *Light After a Layoff*, which she wrote when she was Dawn Mitchell. I met her on a flight as I returned from a job interview. The book title caught my attention because I had been laid off four months earlier, and it wasn't the first time. I told her a bit about myself and what had happened to me, and Dawn said she'd send me a copy of her book after she got home.

I asked her, "Does your book address being laid off after 55 years of age?"

"No, it doesn't," she replied, "but we do need to talk."

I ended up calling her, and we entered into a formal coaching engagement. She was unique because she coached from a spiritual perspective. That was important to me because of my Christian background, upbringing, and strong, personal faith. After our initial session, Dawn instructed me to read her book before our next meeting. I read it cover to cover, and I was reminded that faith is having the confidence and assurance that anyone should relentlessly and ethically pursue while living one's best life unapologetically. I learned that most people going through a layoff are thinking, "I need that next job to pay my bills, to do this, and to do that." Yet when they proceed that way, they tend to lower their sights, devaluing their worth and potential career growth trajectory. Without a paradigm shift, the greatness that all of us have inside of us is muffled and eventually becomes mediocre. "You don't want to digress," Dawn told me in our coaching sessions. "You have a good background. All layoffs are not your fault, but they are a crossroad where you need to find your direction or redirect yourself onto the right path. You have to accept the fact that things happen for a reason."

I really needed to hear that, considering I have been laid off no less than three times over the past decade after being stable for the previous 25-plus years of my professional life.

It was a little daunting. She said of my initial job loss, "The one thing you did with that first one was you got stuck in the grieving process. You did not push through and get back up and start doing what you needed to do." That entire layoff lasted five months and was the longest of the trio, and she hit the nail on the head. Dawn coached me about the impact of the regime change and how, due to the short tenure I had in that organization, I probably wasn't as connected as I would have been had I been there for three years. Things happen that are sometimes out of your control. She encouraged me to not feel sorry for myself, stop looking backward, and instead look forward at what I could do differently now and how I could continue to grow.

I spent several sessions with Dawn and still meet with her today. Her approach to coaching is simple. She speaks from the content in her book, reads a Bible scripture here and there, and prays before and after every session. With the new direction I'm now headed in, I am experiencing the fruits of her coaching and its timeless message to progress, not regress. I know I have a lot to offer, and one of the evidences of that realization is my decision to contribute to this book. I have two rows of books on the bookshelf in my office packed from one end to the other with mentoring, coaching, and talent development books. I'll often pick one, read a couple chapters, put it down, and do something at work that raises a question, and I'll think, "I've got a book on that." Later, I'll go home, pick up that book, and start role playing from it—and to think I'm now contributing to such a book? It's exciting and indicative of the new journey I'm undertaking.

The Purpose and Power of Mentorship

When I look at what I feel puts me ahead of the pack when working with others, it's my relevant, related experience as a leadership consultant. There are very few, I believe, who can coach or mentor exactly as I can on that topic from a relevancy perspective. One of my most successful clients was Erica. When I take on any new client, I believe it is essential to ensure that my clients understand their responsibility to shape their career. Erica has always been committed to making an impact and was willing to do the work necessary to drive her career forward. With that mindset in place, she initiated discussions to help facilitate her growth in the organization, which later reminded me of the very thing Dawn coached me to do when I was laid off: to think outside the box and to define a career trajectory that transcends what happens from organization to organization. This is vital for professionals since organizations regularly go through changes associated with leadership, the economy, and mergers.

Erica was always enthusiastic about a new chapter in her career, but she did not always recognize when it was time to turn the page. During annual reviews, layoffs, and other related setbacks, we should always try to discern when it is time to move on. I helped Erica pinpoint strengths that would bode well for her career in the present and in the future. We regularly reviewed her resume against her brand and worked on interview prep and negotiations on job offers. Today, Erica is a leader in a major company, and she is empowering her staff using methods I taught her. Being a man of faith, I believe we are told to plant seeds and they will multiply, and as a coach with Erica and others, I create a community where "iron sharpens iron" (Proverbs 27:17) as they help one another improve.

As I compare the difference between coaching and mentoring, I believe mentoring speaks *to* you, tries to help you along, and provides advice, while coaching speaks *for* you, listens to what you say, and drives you to do and make the decisions on your own. One of the big companies that I worked for had a phrase for mentorship programs: "It's your career. You drive." That's the approach I take. You need to have thoughts on where you want to go and what you want to be, and from a mentorship perspective, I can then help you formulate your ideas, take them to the next level, and guide you. As a coach, I ask a lot of questions to pull out of you what you may be hiding or scared to divulge. It is that deeper dive through mentoring that then brings out those things that are not on the surface and addresses them. I have mentored a lot of students and young career folks in engineering and other majors. I'm most proud of Thomas, a young man who was pursuing an interesting dual major of aerospace engineering and accounting. He was torn between working for a company or starting his own business after graduation. We met for several phone sessions to formulate his thoughts and ideas to help him frame what success looked like and what he enjoyed doing. He ended up launching a successful branding and web development business while working part-time for a small engineering services business, satisfying both of his desires.

When I evaluate a potential client as to whether that person is the best candidate for coaching or for mentoring, I address early on if they have had previous mentoring or coaching, as well as try to get their perspective on the difference between the two. A lot of people will quickly claim, "Oh, yeah, I've had many mentors," but they don't say they have had many coaches. But it wasn't until I really understood what mentoring and coaching were that I could appreciate

The Purpose and Power of Mentorship

a good mentor versus a bad one. Interestingly, when I look back at the mentors I had in the past, I gained more value from people that were on a tangential path with mine. In other words, they diverged professionally from what I was currently doing. So, when I was an engineer, my best mentors came from program management, finance, or accounting. I understood the real perk of being able to mentor with people who weren't in my chain of command or in my field. I learned the most from them because they could talk to me about what it is like to be "over there," and how taking that off-ramp could also provide an on-ramp back to engineering or whatever else was my focus at that particular time.

This broadened my perspective—such as when I mentored with a colleague who served as vice president of programs. The one thing he talked about was that there are not many program managers who possessed the technical knowledge I had. He said that would be an asset and help pave the way for me to grow into the corporate management arena. At the same time, he cautioned me on the downside, which was the challenge of being able to address my technical approach in a way that would be understood by others. It gave me an opportunity to work on my delivery, and it provided an opportunity to really dig into the finer points of project management.

As I have been mentored or coached, and, in turn, have mentored or coached others, I have found that the biggest barriers to success that exist in people's minds are themselves and the fear of failure. We tend to put obstacles in our own way. I went through some training in the early 1990s at the Creative Center

All Things Happen for a Reason

for Leadership in Greensboro, North Carolina. It was called "The Looking Glass Experience," and it focused on getting to see yourself the way others see you. One of the reasons I went there was because I was outspoken and a bit assertive. I'm not a little guy, about five-eleven-and-a-half and 220 pounds, and the way I presented myself was seen by others as being assertive, in part because of my physical size. I didn't perceive myself that way, but it's not what I see, but how others see me, that matters. After the training, I saw a psychiatrist to better understand the feedback. One of the things that was discussed was that we have to learn to navigate around the obstacles that we put in front of ourselves. My obstacle was my failure to acknowledge and identify my blind spots. Ignoring or not showing empathy is a fear-avoiding tactic that I did not see and needed to recognize. The fear of failure, meanwhile, is sometimes driven by the organizational culture we're in, or by familiar conditions or internal biases on the proper way to navigate in business. If that culture does not allow for failure, or for the lessons that failure brings to develop the faith to know you can fail and continue on, then you'll stop trying after getting shot down a few times. I did exactly that a few times in my career. It wasn't a long-term thing, but it was difficult. Another concern is that you can get complacent and not want to keep trying, so you end up getting stale. Then, when the time comes to market yourself internally or externally for another opportunity, you don't have anything to promote.

When I look back on my life and upbringing, I was raised by my mother, Cleo, the owner of a small confectionary business, and my father, Amos, a licensed master electrician and contractor. I attended private school from first through twelfth grade, then went on to Tuskegee Institute to earn a bachelor's in electrical engineering. My father was a driven perfectionist and hard on me. Though both my parents are deceased, I can still hear my father tell me, "You must be better than me. If you don't want to go to college, get on the truck. Let's go to work. My mother was my rock and safe haven who also pushed hard work. Both led by example and inspired me to relentlessly pursue the engineering field. Because of that, I have achieved what I am today.

As a mentor and coach, I use what I learned and gained from them, other lessons learned in life, and the benefit of hindsight to identify what I may have contributed to the circumstances I have faced, look at the feedback I received, and discern how I can use that to help someone else move forward in their situation. My parents taught me that work ethic was paramount, but I don't see that in a lot of people today, even in some who I mentor and coach. In those cases, we have to have a conversation about the background of their parents and what they did growing up. If they don't have a strong work ethic in their DNA, I can't coach it into them. What I've found is that a lot of them are first- or second-generation college graduates who didn't have a work ethic role model in their lives. For them, school was viewed as the way out from having to learn a hard work ethic.

Another lesson I've learned at each organization I've worked for is, before doing anything else, I need to understand the culture, figure out who I can trust, and decide who I can count on from my peers. When I first got out of college, someone told me how I needed to "learn the system" wherever I worked, and I realize I tended to lose some of that focus as I progressed professionally. Knowing the system, being strategic, and using a methodical approach is vital to initiating the changes you want to make in yourself and the company that employs you.

After that, you need to sell the change, get buy-in from your colleagues, and incrementally put it into place.

To anyone who wants to become a mentor to others, you need to establish a strong foundation by being really good and deep in some area of expertise. That is what you bring to the table and can offer people—and don't be afraid to enroll in the school of hard knocks to get that *something* in your toolbox that people can see as being valuable to them.

It's just as Dawn Owens taught me: all things happen for a reason. Push through, get back up, and start doing what you need to do, and you'll make a significant impact in the lives of others.

Dwayne Simpson is the founder of DND Global Enterprises, LLC, an executive coaching, leadership consultant, and recruiting firm. Dwayne brings straight talk, often unconventional perspectives, and the depth of his executive experience to his coaching, consulting, and mentoring. Dwayne's experience spans multiple top 10 aerospace and defense corporations in progressive leadership roles, and he has been involved in corporate diversity and inclusion councils. Contact Dwayne at dwayne@dndglobalenterprises.com

2

The Thriving of Mankind

Valeene Bedford

MY MOM, EFFIE Mae, always hated it.
"You brought home somebody else?" she'd say, hands on hips. "I told you not to bring anyone home."
I'd shrug and smile at the person next to me. "This kid has no other friends. Everybody is bullying this kid. They need a friend."
I was always dragging folks home, much to mom's exasperation. I couldn't help it. It was who I was—and still am. Caring for others who are disadvantaged and forming relationships with them is not only an extension of my Christian faith, it is one of the foundational aspects of being a mentor and doing mentorship.
Taking it a step further, I believe mentoring is based in an innate desire to ensure the continuity and thriving of mankind. We have an internal sense of the need to transfer critical knowledge. If you've ever sat with an elder whose conversation automatically shifts into a transference-of-wisdom mode, you've experienced it. We also

possess an awareness of our individual eldership whose wisdom must be passed on to others. It's an intrinsic part of our humanity.

My parents, as natural mentors, certainly embodied this. I can still recall mom saying to us as youngsters, "I'm not raising children. I'm raising adults!" This was usually on the heels of some instruction being explained as purposeful for a desired result that was meant to hone us for that outcome. She was embracing her eldership awareness: always guiding, correcting, and goading us to a straighter, pre-determined path while establishing clear goals for our relationship. I can't tell you how proud I felt when she told me, "Okay, *you* know everything!" (It was years before I realized she was being sarcastic!)

It's no wonder then that, after retirement from managing an insurance program at a major utility, I created The Mentoring Program in Tucson, Arizona for disadvantaged high school youth in 2017. It was in response to the pleas of a friend who is an assistant principal. He asked me to help get his academically distracted students reoriented to graduation and success beyond high school. I was already teaching acculturation and poverty alleviation skills to adult refugees in my role as co-founder of the Refugee Resource Center. The Center develops educational services, business partnerships for job training and internships, and advocacy assistance for Tucson's extensive refugee population. I simply tweaked our adult resource building program to fit the needs of high school students headed to college. We then partnered with a young professional women's group to enlist mentors for the students, and our Mentoring Program was off to the races.

The Thriving of Mankind

All of that, in addition to being a speaker, educator, and an ordained Christian minister and assistant pastor, has informed my life motto to "know your purpose and live intentionally." It's a motto whose theme I work to convey to every person I teach.

It's interesting that I have such a passion for mentoring, in that I've come to realize that I haven't actually been formally mentored much in my life. My pastor, Anthony Moss, is the most formal mentor I've had aside from my parents. He has a true pastor's heart in that he's always giving, ready to assist, and going the distance with someone most would have dropped much sooner. As senior pastor, he's also a natural mentor of the leaders in the church. He's been a consistent religious mentor for me as an instructor, preacher, and pastor. Incrementally, he has offered me challenging roles that have pushed me to expand my horizons in areas both inside and outside the ministry. Mentors should eventually be able to assess the character and potential of the mentored. It will help mentees to envision achieving more than they would have had the mentor not been a factor in their life.

I guess I've always had my hands in different things. It's not that I want to be busy. I just am. There's this energy inside to make things happen. That's certainly part of what motivates me as a mentor. Early in life I realized that I have been given a number of gifts that should be used, not for self-promotion but to enrich the lives of others. I'm convinced we are here for a purpose greater than ourselves, and we must search for it with all our heart. When we find that purpose, we have a duty to live it. I'm also motivated by the belief that every person has value. There is treasure in everyone, and as humans, we are most satisfied when we can put our hands to a thing and bring something out of it that manifests our treasure within.

Another important aspect of mentoring is that it transcends age. I teach others that they should always be mentoring three groups: those younger, one's peer group, and those older. If we adhered to this, there would be more respect for wisdom received from unexpected places. Many years ago, as the youth pastor at our church, I enlisted the help of Johari and Marianne, a couple of University of Arizona college students. I figured they could help me in relating to the needs of young teens, two of which were my own children. Johari and Marianne were invaluable to us. They were hip and intellectual, with the finesse of youth and the heart to take the necessary risks to reach the children where they were socially and emotionally. Through their influence, we attended Alvin Ailey dance presentations, spent weekends on California college campuses, and even hosted a citywide sex education conference! Our youth group grew beyond our capacity as we created weekly meetings that were wildly interactive, creative, fun—and effective! To this day, I receive feedback from those youth shouting out their appreciation for the job we did in teaching them solid values and standards that are sustaining them in a world gone wild.

After a couple of years, Johari asked me to be her mentor. Admittedly, I didn't have a clue at the time as to what I should do for her in such a role. She was heading off to Ohio State University to earn a master's degree in education, and I was working in a non-managerial role at a local utility. Yet, I acquiesced to her request and did my best to assist in meeting her education-related needs and to provide intellectual stimulation for this deep thinker/poet via our frequent .aol emails. (Yeah, it was *that* long ago!) Johari went on to become a master teacher and is now married with two young children of her own. In a recent women's Bible class, I used her as an example of a wise married woman. After the class, I happened to look at my cellphone and noticed she'd acknowledged me on Facebook as a woman who had enriched her life with solid wisdom on marital relationships, guidance she said she still found to be immensely valuable. Marianne is now a college librarian, and the three of us keep in contact, sharing knowledge and continuing to learn from one another as we teach others.

A mentor can perform a number of roles in the life of a mentee: guide, facilitator, instructor, soundboard, expert, and encourager/cheerleader. The key to a successful experience is establishing from the outset 1) what the mentee *and* the mentor expect to get out of the relationship (know your purpose) and 2) frequently assessing the partnership to see that those expectations are being met (live intentionally). A mentor shouldn't play all of those roles at the same time, however, so I work with each mentee to come up with a mission statement for our engagement right at the beginning. It defines what they are trying to accomplish and works to ensure they stay within the parameters of that mission. The mentor is leading the relationship from the start, and should be prepared to be open, truthful, and respectful. One of the refugee families we assist has six children, four of which are young boys and men ages seven through 20. As is so often the case, all are amazingly bright, though the traumas of their young lives don't always allow that to show in their school grades. As I spend time with them listening and observing, their intellect is keenly apparent. Fifteen-year-old Deo is a very promising young man who makes good grades except in a couple of subjects for which he's not receiving tutoring. We were able to connect him with Travis, a young military specialist who is married and the father of two small daughters.

After preparing Travis, Deo, and his mother for the mentoring process, I left them alone for a couple of weeks. When I checked back, I discovered that Travis had done far more than expected. He had taken all four of the sons under his wing! They'd spent time on the military base playing basketball, and they had planned a hike for the following weekend. On those hiking trails, Travis was able to have introspective talks with the boys, sharing his life story and getting to know them and their needs better. Since he's been mentoring them, the boys have developed plans for their lives, and they are doing better in school. Travis is fulfilled in having a positive impact on the lives of a family of boys and men while satisfying his desire to provide substantive help in the community.

The expectation of mentorship is that both parties will get something out of the relationship that enables each person to focus and grow. I explain the benefits of the mentoring relationship to each mentee and ask him or her to think about what it is they want to get out of that relationship. I also talk about how the mentee is going to reap *social capital*, the importance of which I cannot emphasize enough. Social capital must be cultivated to produce relationships that meet the needs of the mentee. This is usually expressed as, "It's not *what* you know, but *who* you know." There's a lot of truth in that. Once anyone has the tools to navigate their desired future, they'd do well to have someone help them along the way. Having good social relationships with people who are willing to open doors mentees otherwise wouldn't be able to breach is a very important benefit of being mentored.

Early in my career, I worked with Brenda, a dynamic professional with a fierce intellect and a memory like a steel trap. She became an unexpected supporter and sponsor. Brenda was Vice President of Commercial Lending at what was then known as Valley National Bank. I worked as one of her account executive assistants. Though not a formal mentor, Brenda appreciated the breadth of my potential and interests. While working for her at the bank, I started a catering business on the side and informed Brenda as a courtesy. I was soon spending as many hours catering after work as I did at my day job. Brenda recognized my entrepreneurial ambitions, and rather than try to dissuade me, she began to introduce me to her contacts around town. Through her referrals, I catered for a variety of wonderful groups, including the University of Arizona women's basketball team. That's social capital.

There are two qualities absolutely essential for a successful mentoring relationship. One is respect for the individuals involved. This includes their time, their views, and their voice. The second quality is the ability to communicate with truthfulness. As I coordinate mentorship opportunities for The Mentoring Program, it takes clear communication and passion to help the participating mentor and mentee see the vision for what we are working to achieve in bringing them together.

Dee Dee was a senior at my friend's high school and a participant in The Mentoring Program. She was a thoughtful, introspective young woman and was an acknowledged leader even without working to be seen as one. Her goal at the start of the program was to become a police officer. Part of our training involves having the participants look at all the career paths associated with what they want to become, and what it takes academically to achieve those positions. They are taught to research where schooling or training is offered for the positions, the salary as it relates to geography, and the cost of living in those locales. We also work to connect them with a leader in that industry. I introduced Dee Dee to Michelle, a lieutenant who works in the office of the Chief of Police and had offered me her assistance for mentoring. The lieutenant graciously scheduled a meeting for Dee Dee to tour all the departments at police headquarters. Michelle introduced Dee Dee to one of the department's female community resource officers, a former military officer who also wanted to work with youth interested in a career in law enforcement. With their help, Dee Dee learned about the police force and the opportunities available to her.

Dee Dee had always told us she would take a year off to travel after high school graduation and go to college afterward. At the end of her senior year, armed with the realities of her research and the experience with her mentors, she instead decided to join the military to prevent being saddled with insurmountable loans at the end of her college studies. Dee Dee joined the armed forces in the summer of 2019. Her plan is to return to Tucson and eventually become the chief of police.

———

At The Mentoring Program, I give direction in mentor-mentee matches to ensure everyone knows what it is they are supposed to do. I also assess the mentorship throughout the engagement to make sure they are achieving the goals they established at the beginning. We often have to take a step back, look at it, tweak it, and sometimes, even walk away from it.

Partnering mentors with mentees can be a challenging process. I connected a young man with one of our partners, the owner of an area heating and cooling company, who agreed to provide paid, on-the-job training. The young man went to the initial meeting, but then never showed up again. That scenario can be difficult because it could cost us valuable partnerships and impact the mentee's desire to try again when they are better prepared for such a process. I've since learned from that experience. We convinced the young man to enter Job Corps. Gratefully, the partnership remains intact because our matches are with compassionate business owners or organizational leaders who want to do good for less fortunate people. I don't want to lose good mentors because I didn't assess either party carefully enough. That hasn't happened often, but it's always a possibility because mentees are by nature traversing new territory, growing, and learning. There will be a wrong turn here or there. After all, if they weren't expected to make one, a mentor wouldn't be needed.

It is also important to match mentors and mentees based on their personality and values. For example, if one or the other is not aware of cultural complexities, that can interfere with the mentor's goals or advice, causing a breakdown in the ability of that relationship to produce the desired result. It is vital to acknowledge the social and psychological impacts of such distinctions in this country, and this advice can likely translate to any other country. If someone misjudges or prejudges something along those lines, they stand the chance of offending the other person.

Alaynna is from the islands of the Bahamas. She is earthy, passionate, a social activist, and poetic: singer-songwriter Erykah Badu and poet Maya Angelou rolled into one young, mature sista. Alaynna has witnessed more than her share of social and family turmoil, yet her power still rises. An outspoken, dedicated member of The Mentoring Program, it was soon apparent that she needed to be paired with a mentor who "got" her unapologetic, total self. Enter Michaela. She is, in a word, pastoral. Michaela takes in lambs of every type, along with all their stuff, and then shepherds them against all odds. She became the perfect mentor for Alaynna, whose mother was a nurse and worked weekends. When home, Alaynna's mom frequently responded to her in frustration, unable to understand her daughter's newfound American ease in exercising the right that allows a woman to speak freely in society. Michaela is my middle daughter and the founder of Black Girl Vibranium, the organization that provided the initial group of mentors for our program. She attended one of our program sessions, which are designed to allow organic mentor relationships to flourish between the monthly guest speakers and the students. When Michaela heard Alaynna's need beyond her stated desire to attend church weekly, she began to pick Alaynna up for church that very week and each Sunday thereafter. She included Alaynna in her family time and listened non-judgmentally when Alaynna needed to psychologically and spiritually *breathe*. As a soundboard and encourager, Michaela successfully helped Alaynna navigate the path of a creative young person who simply needed an understanding, listening ear and wise counsel when a busy parent seemed so far away.

The Mentoring Program is designed to do more than just pair the students with mentors. In our work with high school children, we teach a broad range of life skills such as how to speak in different settings, the power of voice and community, and recognizing economic predators. We also train on how to create a budget, determining earnings needed while in or out of school, and interviewing for an employment position. In addition, we show students how to select an appropriate college for their chosen field of interest and where to live based on career viability.

We invite a mentor to attend a meeting each month. For an hour, they share about themselves and whatever they desire to impart into the lives of the children. They then invite the participants to contact them if they desire. We maintain a pool of potential mentors through Black Girl Vibranium and our statewide business partnerships throughout Arizona.

The Purpose and Power of Mentorship

After someone is matched with a mentee, we provide a short training on how to structure the relationship. One young lady was matched with a physical therapist, one of two career paths she wanted to explore. The therapist provided an unpaid internship where she could work a couple of days a week to train directly with his patients. Although she had just graduated from high school, she worked alongside other physical therapists-in-training from the University of Arizona Institute for Sports Medicine.

We do the same for our refugee clients at the Refugee Resource Center. With the help of Randiesia Fletcher, my partner and co-founder at that organization, the center matches refugees with individuals and organizations that can help them with whatever they want to do to become independent and self-sustaining. At times, we create the curriculum and process, then do our own training or bring in volunteer specialists to teach. We are a 100 percent volunteer organization and, amazingly, it works. Not long after we'd been open, Randiesia met Bill, an engineer. He and his wife had spent many years abroad due to his work throughout Africa before returning to live in California. When we met Bill, they had sold their home and moved to Tucson. Though Bill still had an office and staff in California, he shared his strong desire to help refugees here. Randiesia and I had a number of refugee friends who had been engineers in their homelands but were now working as dishwashers, caregivers, and in other menial, entry-level positions. Bill was a Godsend. He agreed to join us as a volunteer engineering instructor, and our Fundamentals of Engineering (FOE) class was created. Randiesia and Bill wrote the curriculum, and Bill taught the class along with Dr. Garcia, an engineer educated in Mexico and a university professor. Another Muslim friend, Fatima, a University of Arizona engineering student from Pakistan, also assisted and led the study group classes each Wednesday. When our students graduated the class 16 weeks later, they were ready to take the FOE certification exam. Those who passed were then able to work in engineering positions. We witnessed the first graduates go from earning $11.00 an hour (minimum wage at the time) to $35.00 an hour. Those students never looked back as their families were instantly raised to a sustainable income. After a few semesters, our class gained such notoriety that the University of Arizona picked it up, with our blessing, as a continuing education course. Bill has continued to mentor one of the students, Hasim from Iraq, and employed him at his new Tucson office.

Good mentoring isn't hard. It just takes commitment, clear communication, and frequent assessment to ensure everyone is receiving what they want to get out of it. Honesty and openness allow both parties to gain growth from the experience.

Mentoring is a beautiful way to leave a legacy. It doesn't even require any monetary expense, just quality time and a willingness to help. The rewards are beyond fantastic when you see a life change because you took the time to share your treasure with another. People know when you care, and for many, that's all they need to get to the next level. Many of us don't have a foundation through which we can impact lives for generations. We may even feel that any monetary help sent to some near or faraway cause is but a proverbial drop in the bucket, of little value where there are so many needs. Trust me, your drop matters. But when you become a mentor, your gift will indeed be felt across generations. It impacts everything that emanates from the mentee's life. I see it as the melding of two lives on a path to keep humanity on track and thriving. It is the answer to that question that has challenged us through the ages: "Am I my brother's keeper?"

Mentoring answers with a resounding, "Yes!"

Valeene Bedford is an ordained Christian minister and assistant pastor of a non-denominational church in Tucson, Arizona. After retirement from corporate life in 2017, she created The Mentoring Program for disadvantaged high school youth, and in 2020 she extended the program to K-8 students. Valeene was selected as the University of Arizona Black Alumni's Woman of the Year in 2011 for her service to the community. Contact Valeene at profvbedford@gmail.com

3

Rite of Passage

Daniel Scott

THE WORD "MENTOR" originated about 750 B.C., the approximate time when the Greek poet, Homer, wrote *The Odyssey*. The character named Mentor was a trusted friend, one who taught and gave help and advice.

Today, just as it was then, knowledge is passed on to someone less experienced, or, in some cases, younger. As such, my first experience with mentoring was with my parents, aunts and uncles, and my extended family—and it was mentorship by example using a most unusual method.

Every summer, my parents, Daniel Sr. and Cora, took a vacation from parenting. My siblings and my cousins all came together to stay at my parent's house for two weeks. Next, we'd all go to stay with my Uncle Tommy and Aunt Bobbie for the next two weeks. After that, we headed off to stay another two weeks with my Aunt Evelyn and Uncle Snook. On a given summer, depending upon the ages of my siblings and cousins, there could be up to 15 or more family members traveling from house to house over those six weeks.

Being thrown together like that, we thrived as we took care of each other and influenced one another. To this day, my brothers, sisters, and cousins are as close as ever. We really don't call ourselves cousins. We're like brothers and sisters. Without knowing it, we were, in a very real sense, mentoring each other as we learned from one another. I'll never forget the summer I was involved in a hit-and-run motorcycle accident. I was 13, and my younger cousin, Stephanie, took care of me. While I was in a body cast for several months, she nurtured me back to health, including teaching me how to walk again. Stephanie was selfless and encouraged me more than I could ever hope. The first time I had to stand up in the full body cast, I passed out. I was in traction. All I could do was stand up and lay down. But with help from her, and the rest of the family, I didn't miss a beat as I still traveled to my aunt's and uncle's homes during that summer. I have a memento in my office, a Julius Irving signed and autographed basketball, which recalls that same summer when the Philadelphia 76ers won the NBA championship with Dr. J. at the helm. That ball, though, will always remind me of Stephanie.

In the end, it was all about family. We might have fought one another for toys, food, or clothes, but woe to anybody who messed with any one of us. Today, we are all grown and have our own kids, and we believe in our family motto of having "a fruitful life in the service of our family as well as others."

Since my first mentors were my family, I believe mentorship is personal, and it's all about trust. When my parents

Rite of Passage

were away, my family passed on their knowledge to each other. They did so with the objective of preparing each of us to take accountability for everything that happens in our lives and to take responsibility for our purpose in life. I know that I am the product of every experience that I have had in the past, now have in the present, and will have in the future.

Purpose, actually, is such a beautiful yet simple thing. There is such power in purpose. I recently attended a leadership course with people from all over the world. One of the assignments was for each person to write down their personal "purpose statement." A person's purpose is similar to their brand, and it is not something to be memorized, but lived. It is what people believe you stand for, and we have to be careful that there isn't a misalignment between what we think, and the actions, abilities, behavior, and attitudes we exhibit. Those are the things that other people see. Purpose requires a great deal of thought. It is not necessarily just the vision of where you want to be or the mission of how you get there. Purpose is all encompassing.

With that in mind, my purpose statement is "to influence and inspire others to live in their purpose, so they can be better for themselves, their families, their communities, and the world." From that, I am convinced that mentoring has the ability to create a better person, a better team, a better organization, a better business, and, therefore, a better world.

I see mentoring as a three-stage rite of passage. It begins first with *separation*. It's a realization that you need to withdraw from the group or peers where you currently reside and seek someone from outside your network who can pass on their knowledge to you. This allows you to acquire information and nurture relationships that will cause you to detach from your former self.

Secondly, there is a *transfer of information* where learning is achieved as someone more seasoned gives support and guidance to you who are less seasoned. This step goes back to trust, in that it is a very personal act to ask someone to help shape who you are and influence your career and then allow them to do so.

The third stage is the *transition of knowledge into wisdom*. Wisdom is knowledge put into practice, and it is through having learned new skills and insights that you can seize opportunities to apply that knowledge to your life and vocation. This is where you once had trouble controlling your emotion but now exhibit the ability to respond to crisis rather than react to it; where you begin to understand your impact and how to increase your value to your boss, co-workers, and customers; where you recognize situations before they occur, anticipate a course of action, and implement the right outcome. It's where the student becomes the teacher and the mentee shows the mentor new insights.

When I mentor someone, we set up our first discussion to review and determine the scope of the engagement, the cadence we'll keep, and the timeframe we'll need to accomplish what the person wants to achieve. For example, one young team leader, Martin, wanted to learn the art of influential communication. He not only desired for his message to be heard and understood, but that the actions necessary to meet the objective would be carried out by his team in

Rite of Passage

a timely fashion. In our initial sessions, we talked about passion and purpose, personal brands, and various communication styles. At the essence of the conversations was the premise that the foundation of communication has, at its base, a message and a call-to-action. What we found was that his message was clear and understood, but the call-to-action was not being achieved because of real or perceived cultural, gender, racial, and organizational norms. In some cases, it was not even being acted upon. After some data gathering and some soul searching, we realized something very important. Even after communicating the "why" of what needed to be done, the WIIFM ("What's in it for me?") of the message needed to be made clear. It was *how* the message was being communicated that mattered most in this case.

To address the "how" of his communication, we read various chapters from *Kiss, Bow, or Shake Hands* by Terri Morrison and gleaned nuggets of information from *The Definitive Book of Body Language* by Allan and Barbara Pease. This helped Martin enhance his communication. We found that, for his situation, email was best designed to convey status, not communicate in detail. He began placing the purpose and objective at the top of emails to his team to ensure the call-to-action was clear and understood. He also modeled best physical behaviors when communicating.

It was such a turnaround that the mentoring relationship came to an end after he consistently began coming to me with situations that already had alternative solutions and a sound rationale for the solution he thought best addressed the situation. The student had indeed become the teacher, and I was no longer needed as a mentor.

The Purpose and Power of Mentorship

When I engage in mentoring sessions, I have the goal of helping the mentee see for themselves the purpose ("why") and the call-to-action ("how") so they can execute the solution ("what"). Andrea was just starting her technical career when I began mentoring her. After a few summer internships, she told me she had found her professional calling and wanted to be a manager. She had just finished her undergraduate degree and had nearly no professional experience. It was encouraging, but surprising, to me that she had not only found her calling but wanted to immediately be in leadership. We started by discussing her "why," and I learned it was intimately personal for her. She had lost a loved one due to chronic health issues, and she wanted to guide and lead others to become healthier and more informed on matters that affect their physical and mental well-being. Then we looked at "how" this could be accomplished. Andrea did extensive research, talking to several state and local public health officials, doctors, and health professionals to identify the root causes for the health concerns that impacted her community. She also visited hospitals and health centers to talk to those dealing directly with medical challenges. Finally, we went into the "what." Andrea began to partner with local clinics, nurses, and doctors to implement health awareness forums at local community centers, clinics, and schools. Eventually, Andrea realized her calling and became a health manager/coordinator at a nonprofit organization. Today she continues to do the work she believes she is meant to do.

I truly believe mentoring Andrea benefitted me the most because she was from a younger generation—the story of

The Odyssey brought to life for me—and I found that her and I face the same challenges despite our generational gap, just in different ways. We still shared some of the same thoughts and processes. In her case, Andrea changed from a technical career to one that best fit with the fulfillment of her "why." Things don't have to go the way you first thought they would.

When I coach, I am much more deliberate in telling someone what to do based on the objective of the person or group. One of my colleagues, John, aspired to be a director. However, he exhibited behaviors that were not at all director-like. While he was extremely intelligent, he seemingly wanted everyone to know he was the smartest guy in the room. Therefore, he did not properly develop those around him and continuously rubbed his team, and sometimes his customers, the wrong way. John had quite a few peer and executive mentors when he asked me to coach him, and I candidly shared my observations with him. Just as important, I revealed how his behavior and attitude (perceived or actual) made me feel. John admitted he was aware of his behavioral issues, but he was not making the changes within himself to meet his directorship goal.

I gave John the book by Daniel Goldman entitled, *Emotional Intelligence: Why It Can Matter More Than IQ*. After years of being passed over for a number of director-level positions, John came to the conclusion that the common denominator for his situation was himself. He began to realize, through reading, learning, and reviewing his impact on others, that he would never reach his goal if he did not adjust. Eventually, John did change, and he achieved his goal. He said it was through intentional discussions with his mentors, coaches, customers, and team (via a 360-degree assessment where feedback was received from his subordinates, colleagues, and supervisors) that he was able to make the modifications necessary to be more director-like in his thoughts, communications, behaviors, and actions.

Most interesting from my coaching with John was how I applied some of what I had learned when I was a football coach and referee while raising my children. I'd tell the team, "Here is the play. Go run it. If you do these things, we'll be successful." Coaching is very deliberate. Just do the things that will make you successful. From that background, I had the ability to actually show John what I saw and describe to him what I felt. "Here's what you say, and here's what I hear and what I see. Do you believe that what you are doing has the impact to get you where you want to be?" It was so fulfilling.

Both mentoring and coaching are equally important and, depending on the situation, are sometimes interchangeable. I believe all successful people need a mentor and a coach as well as an advocate (one who supports or promotes the interests of a cause, an individual, or a group) when advocacy is possible. As opportunities allow, the mentor can often become an advocate for the mentee's next stage of development or career advancement.

I became an advocate when I had a position open as a program manager working at a major engineering company. I intentionally hired Safraz, for whom the assignment itself was a stretch. Safraz had great skill in engineering and operations. He was extraordinarily passionate about changes and execution, attributes you want to see in a program manager. But he had not yet exhibited any competencies in program management to be able to actually lay out a plan, lead, influence, and execute. Skills can be taught, but you can't teach passion, attitude, or behavior. Safraz exhibited all three of those, and because he did, he met the challenges that came with the new role and learned lessons that brought growth. When the time came for Safraz to prepare for other roles within the organization, I had the ability to advocate on his behalf, providing an avenue by which he could build a toolbox that he could use to exceed and excel in positions of higher authority.

Safraz went on to become a vice president. We are not only colleagues. We are friends—and we now have the ability to advocate for one another.

When I look at my current mentoring experiences with colleagues in comparison to my initial mentoring experiences with my family, I think they both are a means to an end. With my family experiences, a series of fundamental competencies were instilled in me that helped shape the person I have become. I am fortunate to continue to be shaped by my family as they continue to care enough about me to help me grow mentally, spiritually, and physically. The current mentoring experiences I share with mentors and mentees are an extension of those previous experiences. At the end of the day, the person—be it me or those who I mentor—will have the tools to make progress in their lives, their workplaces, and their communities.

THE PURPOSE AND POWER OF MENTORSHIP

In the end, no one gets anywhere alone. A fruitful life is one spent in service of others. If I am doing something for someone else, I'm also doing it for myself because it is unselfish and draws me closer to my higher power. I challenge you to do two things: get a mentor and invest in your "self-betterment," and then become a mentor. Continue to invest in yourself by investing in others.

Daniel Scott is a son, brother, uncle, husband, father, coach, mentor, and leader who exists to inspire and influence others to serve their purpose. He is a jack-of-all-trades with 30 years of professional experience including leadership and management in engineering, operations, contracts, general management, business development, and Six Sigma process improvement. Daniel is also a proud submariner who served and qualified on U.S. Navy submarines, and he was an officer in the Civil Engineer Corps. Contact Daniel at dlscottjr1914@yahoo.com

4

An Invaluable Collaboration

Laura Tremaine

ENTREPRENEUR AND AUTHOR Bedros Keulian said it this way: "Take advice from someone who's been there and done that."

Over the course of several years, I've been extremely fortunate to have been mentored by individuals who have achieved a high level of success, and for whom I have tremendous admiration. Each of my mentors has possessed a wealth of knowledge, experience, and wisdom, and each has demonstrated a profound compassion for me and my own unique path in life. It's so true what Ralph Waldo Emerson says: "The only person you are destined to become is the person you decide to be."

I have heartfelt appreciation for the myriad of ways my mentors have generously shared themselves with me. Their willingness to help is humbling and it's a blessing to feel safe enough to communicate with complete candor. The perspective I've received has helped me focus on my own challenges and priorities. Through their gentle questioning and honed listening skills, I have been able to clarify my personal vision of success. Together, we identified pathways to success through proven strategies. My mentors have helped me discover my hidden strengths as well as, admittedly, some hindrances to achieving my life goals.

Not every mentoring or coaching interaction is guaranteed to be inspirational. However, to have the attention of accomplished, talented, and empathetic individuals can truly be life-changing.

I am an example of why mentorship is so vital. It is an invaluable collaboration from which both participants benefit. It has increased my awareness of my role in society and my responsibility to help improve our world. Through my mentors and coaches, I've been able to cultivate a positive work culture as a lending professional and help my team identify their individual strengths. I have learned to encourage the best in them in much the same way I was encouraged. The results have occurred organically and my relationships with my friends, co-workers, and family have deepened as a result. I'm also able to better express the empathy and compassion I've always felt for others, and I've become a more patient and careful listener. There are few things more important in life.

While attending a business conference years ago, I was discussing my goals with the president and CEO of my company. Just then, Justin Tulman, one of the top producing loan officers in the country, walked by. My CEO introduced me to Justin and then spontaneously asked if he might consider mentoring me. Justin enthusiastically agreed, and we set up a schedule for monthly mentoring calls from his office in Massachusetts to mine in Arizona.

At first, I didn't know what to expect, but Justin immediately dove into the deep end. He asked me what specific goals I

An Invaluable Collaboration

hoped to accomplish that year, and then shared what steps he felt would be most effective to accomplish them. He welcomed all my questions and openly shared some of his best practices when dealing with clients and referral partners. During my year of coaching with Justin, I received a promotion, and it was Justin who helped me navigate through my new responsibilities. Justin nurtured our relationship (including handwritten notes, congratulatory gifts, etc.) while showing me, through example, the reasons for his immense success. He was always honest, caring, completely transparent, and generous beyond measure. It's been said that "trust is earned when actions meet words," and I simply couldn't trust Justin more.

I was one of the first to be formally mentored within our organization— and my company has since launched IGNITE, a full coaching platform. To this day, I'd happily climb a mountain to help Justin in any way, and I am honored to call him my friend. In 2019, Justin closed over $100 million of production for our company, an outstanding achievement which simply couldn't happen to a nicer guy.

Writer and statesman Johan Wolfgang von Goethe wrote, "Everything is hard before it is easy." I understand well the grit, hard work, and perseverance necessary for achievement as I have faced numerous personal and professional challenges. For many years, I was vice president of international development for a U.S.-based franchise system. I lost that position shortly after the terrorist attacks of September 11, 2001 when international commerce stalled—and I was subsequently forced to reinvent myself. This marked an extremely challenging time in my life, full of uncertainty and fear. I felt a bit lost. Looking back, I realize how much the clarity of a mentor or coach would've helped me then with some of the immediate and difficult choices I faced.

I took an interim job to pay the bills. I was in the middle of a large home remodeling project which was running significantly over budget. I knew I was hard-working and capable, and accepted with humility the necessity to keep learning and expanding my skills. I placed one foot in front of the other and pushed through my self-doubt and insecurities. I then adopted the mindset that, when necessary, I could "outwork" anyone. I learned that failure is one of our greatest teachers, and that *all* successful people have experienced and overcome a multitude of failures and rejections. But, at that time in my life, I didn't have the wisdom to understand (let alone embrace) the knowledge that the more we fail, the more we grow. Writer Katherine MacKenett aptly said, "Now, every time I witness a strong person, I want to know: What darkness did you conquer in your story? Mountains do not rise without earthquakes."

As I struggled to professionally reinvent myself, a friend, Yvette Villamana, asked if I might be interested in helping her as she started a new company. A super high-level professional who needed someone to be her personal assistant, I accepted and proceeded to do a myriad of tasks for my friend, some quite menial. This woman ultimately became the catalyst for my current profession, which I passionately love, and I often wonder what my path might've been if I had been unwilling to be humble and "do what it takes." Yvette is still a close and cherished friend as well as a true life coach. I learned from her to stay humble and stay hungry.

Our growth can indeed be forced by a change in circumstances, whether personal or professional. However, it can

An Invaluable Collaboration

also be chosen by ourselves and/or encouraged by others. I've learned through mentoring that these challenging times are, in fact, our best learning moments. Tough times also teach us gratitude. I firmly believe that even during difficult times, the more grateful you are, the happier you will be. Remember, there are many people who would love to have your bad days. Stay grateful. Additionally, you will get the most out of your mentoring when you begin the relationship and process with gratitude. Prior to a scheduled session with your mentor or coach, organize your thoughts and prepare notes for topics of conversation that are time sensitive. I've always set aside a particular notebook for my coaching sessions; it's great to look back and review later.

All of my formal, paid mentors have lived out of state, so we had regularly scheduled phone or video calls. Each session was approximately one hour and took place once or twice a month. These appointments were etched in stone well in advance. I gave these calls all of my focus and attention. Initially, I was given behavioral assessments and was asked lots of questions. This was a guided process designed to help me put the pieces together for myself. I continue to be provided suggested reading lists and online tools for effectiveness in my verbal and non-verbal communication, as well as tracking devices to facilitate accountability and progress. Tracking is essential because you can't manage what you can't measure. I have been led through the process of creating life and business plans that included goal setting, action steps for reaching the next level, and methods to monitor my progress in areas specific to my profession.

My coaches and I often reviewed and refined daily disciplines. Specifically, they taught me how to implement

The Purpose and Power of Mentorship

consistent daily, weekly, and monthly activities to help assist in reaching my goals, and they have helped with organizational tools, time blocking, delegation, and team building.

It's amazing how much can be covered in a short period of time, and I usually felt the time was efficiently spent. Sometimes we digressed a bit, and that was fine, too. And, of course, I've received lots of encouragement to step outside my comfort zone (because that's where the magic happens) by looking at any recurring patterns that might be self-sabotaging to my success. I love the level of trust each of my coaches earned and the easy banter we developed over time. From them, I discovered how important it is to find our "why" and identify our passions. I also love that my coaches have pushed me to become the best version of myself.

Growth on a personal and professional level requires that we "let go" by adopting a new mindset with the willingness to change our thinking about ourselves, others, and our challenges in life. I have one mentor who sends out a daily inspiration each morning by email. My days begin with one of these affirmations, quotes, or thoughts, and I have interspersed a few of those throughout this chapter. Whenever possible, I also start my day with some quiet reflection and a few minutes of measured breathing and meditation.

One of my mentors introduced me to author and public speaker, Dr. Caroline Leaf. I've heard her speak in person, and I love her podcasts and books. In her presentations on the mind-brain connection, she says that 99 percent of the time we are, in rapid succession, thinking, feeling, and

An Invaluable Collaboration

choosing, and that we have the power to self-regulate our thoughts. This is important because what we think about ultimately impacts us physically and emotionally. Another mentor speaks often about emotions, responses to those emotions, and the importance of kindness and patience. He preaches about the "pause" and taking time to not immediately react to something. That's a mistake I've made far too many times in my life and have always regretted. As entertainer Groucho Marx once said, "Speak when you are angry, and you will make the best speech you will ever regret." Pausing is a true-life skill I recommend to everyone. Some other quick happiness tips shared by one of my mentors are 1) don't listen to gossip, 2) ignore what people say about you (this is so liberating), 3) design your own life, 4) look for the good in every situation, and 5) once it's past, let it go.

Coaching has also helped me tremendously with achieving work-life balance. We live in an incredibly complicated world with technology that keeps us plugged into work for far more than 40 hours a week. Life balance is different for every individual. I used to stress out about the fact that my life wasn't as balanced as I thought it should be, so I allow myself to shift priorities when needed. I don't think we can find balance in our lives without eliminating those things which no longer suit new situations in our lives. Through the years, I've had to change some of daily routines and refocus my time. What worked for me five years ago isn't going to work for me now. So, in working toward my own personal balance, I've learned to narrow my focus and concentrate on top priorities.

When looking at balance, it's also very important to clarify our own core values. What is truly important? Is it wealth, family, success, fun, beauty, spirituality, and so on? It's critical

THE PURPOSE AND POWER OF MENTORSHIP

to look within and determine where your values lie. Essential, too, is to make time for something that brings you happiness. Because I am a bit of a workaholic, I have to block out time for these events on my calendar. This "refresh" time is essential for my balance, and that means I often have to set boundaries and politely decline when asked to do something else during that scheduled time. Keeping a journal has numerous benefits. This practice takes discipline, but it can be an illuminating process in ways that are difficult to describe. It clears out some of the cobwebs in my mind and helps me sleep more peacefully. It's an opportunity for me to be brutally honest about personal struggles and take a moment of pride for a personal success. It stimulates creative flow. Some people illustrate their journals with pictures and graphs, but it can also be a stream-of-consciousness diary. Other personal routines that have helped me tremendously are time spent alone for self-reflection, reading, exercise, enjoying the miracle of nature, contemplative prayer, cooking, gardening, and spending quality time with my family and pets. For years, I believed hard work would make me more productive. I now clearly understand it's a balance of hard work, exercise, healthy eating, sleep, and time off.

Approximately nine years ago, I placed an ad for an assistant that outlined various required skills. It also stated, "Experience in the mortgage business a must." I received a multitude of resumes and scheduled several interviews. One of those resumes was from Erin, who had zero experience in the mortgage business. At first, I put it aside, since

An Invaluable Collaboration

her degree was in philosophy. She was quite shy and would barely make eye contact. However, she followed up with an email emphatically stating she was very capable of learning a high pressure, frenetic industry. She also posted a perfect score on the 10-question quiz I provided each applicant. Erin further stood out through the attitude and approach she took to answering each question. I hired Erin, and it's been a joy to mentor her throughout the years. Erin is smart, organized, and has an amazing work ethic. She's a woman of very few words, yet she has absorbed and implemented my coaching like a sponge. She really took to heart most of what I shared with her. I've watched this shy, young woman evolve into a confident mortgage producer as well as a wonderful wife and mother of two sons. Our personal and professional relationship remains a treasure to me.

When it comes to finding a mentor or coach for yourself, there are many companies which offer formal programs as well as numerous publications, online resources, and webinars. But I think the best place to start is to identify those individuals within your network who you admire and might like to emulate. Think of a few, because the "one" you think might be a perfect fit may not be after all. When you initially meet with potential mentors or coaches, have some notes prepared. After the meeting, send a handwritten note thanking them for their time. After you've identified the individual with whom you have the most connection and whose expertise resonates with the goals you hope to achieve, ask for their help.

Mentorship and coaching can help you evolve as a human being, striving to always be mindful and intentional with your thoughts, words, and actions. I believe each day we are faced with choices and our response to these choices determines the

The Purpose and Power of Mentorship

trajectory of our lives. I want to use the things I've been through to help others and let them know they are not alone. Many of us have the same struggles. Many people contribute to our lives, and sometimes it takes a village. We are all in this together.

I hope you will envision the benefits of having a trusted guide as you face your personal and professional challenges. I encourage you to embrace the possibility of a very bright future. The opportunity for you to collaborate with someone invested in your success is available through mentorship and coaching. With the objective perspective of a mentor, you will be empowered through their wisdom, and you will have meaningful interactions, some of which you'll cherish the rest of your life. Might now be the time to find your "why," ignite your spark, and shape your future?

Laura Tremaine is a lending professional in Tucson, AZ with more than 30 years of experience in local and international business, finance, and lending. Laura brings a wealth of knowledge and extensive experience to her clients and has been recognized throughout the years for her excellence in the industry, most recently included in the top one percent of loan originators in America. Contact Laura at ltremaine@fairwaymc.com

5

Stages and Phases

Lonnie Goodson

AS WE MATURE, I believe every stage of life requires mentorship. Whether it comes from parents, siblings, relatives, pastors, teachers, or supervisors, things change, and you have to be adaptable. A mentor who has experienced and understands those phases can offer suggestions on how you can maneuver through them.

Mentorship is a relationship between two individuals where the mentor shares their knowledge of various subjects based on personal experience, and the mentee receives that knowledge and then introspectively references or adopts that information to enhance their life. A mentor should be prepared to devote their time and energy to the task, and be committed, accountable, and responsible to help their mentee be successful. What you say as a mentor matters and should add value. I also think every mentor has the duty and obligation to teach those from younger generations how to avoid the pitfalls they can face in life.

I grew up in a loving family household in Alabama. My

The Purpose and Power of Mentorship

father, Lonnie, was a farmer and a butcher who had his own farm with livestock. My mother, Ollie, was a "domestic engineer," a stay-at-home mom who did an outstanding job raising me and my two siblings while having ingenuity as an entrepreneur. She established a restaurant and ran it for many years after my father passed away when I was a young teen. I learned a strong work ethic from being there on the farm and from my parents' tireless example.

I was born later in their lives. My brother, Lonzell, was 22 years older than me, so he never lived at home after I came along. My sister, Princetta, though, was 14 years my senior, and I really saw her as the person whose footsteps I wanted to follow. Even when I was a small boy, she taught me to keep up with current affairs, read the paper, and listen to what was happening in the world around me. Princetta was also the first one in our family to go to college, and shortly after she graduated from college, she married her husband, Greg. He didn't have a brother of his own, so he adopted me as his little brother. I learned a lot from Greg about the roles of being a husband, a brother, and a friend. He also provided the example of what it was to be a professional when he worked for Ford Motor Company as a district manager. I see Greg as my first real personal and professional mentor, starting when I was eight and continuing until I was about 21 when he unexpectedly died in a workplace accident.

The three biggest mentorship opportunities in our lives come as we transition through the phases of childhood as we grow up and learn from those around us, our education as we prepare

Stages and Phases

for our profession, and in our profession as we grow and advance in our careers. I have benefitted greatly from being mentored through each one of these stages. It has guided me and strengthened my understanding of the challenges of life. I also seek spiritual mentorship and guidance from my pastor, who has given me valuable lessons about following the leadership of Christ as a husband, father, and electrical engineer.

Two individuals, Jerry Reese and Mike MacKenzie, have meant the most to me as professional mentors. Both are former supervisors who took me under their wings and provided me with the tools I needed to enable my success to soar. Even though they are both retired, I still communicate regularly with them to discuss things going on in my life today.

When I was a young engineer, Jerry was instrumental in teaching me the culture of the company where I was employed and in showing me the do's and don'ts of working in corporate America. He was a mentor throughout the first decade of my professional career at Alcoa Aluminum Company of America. He had been working for that company for about 20 years when I started there, and Jerry understood the ropes and what it meant to come in not only as a new employee, but a black employee, in a predominately Caucasian work environment. This particular area in Indiana had a high presence of white supremacists, and Jerry gave me advice about what to do and say at work and out in the racially charged community. He also helped me with career planning, how to set up a 401(k), how to establish insurance policies for my family, and provided guidance and advice when I bought my first house.

Mike worked for 30 years at the company where I am currently employed. He still understands the tactics and choices the organization makes, what they mean to me, and how I should respond to them. He spoke up for me often and caused other key people to recognize me and my abilities. Mike admired my management style and how I went about accomplishing my work. He sought me out, and I made the decision to work for him and become a program manager under his leadership. He helped me understand how managers and executives think, how to move and advance, and the value of networking and having relationships with other leaders. Finally, Mike had a strong business acumen and I had a strong technical acumen, and together we were able to really perform well for the organization as a team.

My first mentoring opportunity came during high school as I participated in the marching band. As trumpet section leader, I was required to teach the younger musicians how to enhance their performance. They looked up to me and watched how I acted and carried myself.

One of my most significant mentoring opportunities as an adult came taking part in a program to help minorities be better in the workplace. When I was a young professional in the early 1990's, minority employees faced significant disadvantages. Cultural diversity was a big initiative then, but it was not being embraced by lower-level leadership at the company where I was employed. A small organization was established independently, away from the workplace, called The Support and Development Association (SDA). It was created to be a vehicle to help the company overcome the challenges of prejudice and to promote cultural diversity without retaliation. I was a founding member of the SDA, and over the years I mentored many colleagues, several of whom were able to

Stages and Phases

advance in their careers at the company. Today, the SDA is still active and officially recognized throughout the corporation. I am honored to know that I was a part of such a great initiative.

Yvette and A'Shawn were two young ladies who came into the professional and corporate world when cultural diversity was still just being understood. They needed someone to guide them through the process and acclimate them to what the company was doing. As their mentor, I had the opportunity to talk to them about important experiences I'd gone through and how I was able to succeed. Yvette was a young engineer fresh out of college who came into my program back at Alcoa, and I tried to mentor and help her the way Jerry had done with me. A'Shawn was interested in becoming a program manager at my current job, and she came in and did several jobs to build up to that. We met on a monthly basis to talk about her career moves and her next steps, which jobs she should do, and how she should handle a certain manager or situation she might have with another coworker. I gave words of encouragement, advice, and options to consider as she moved forward. Today she has a doctorate degree and is married with a family. They, and others that I have mentored, have achieved many of the goals they desired. Some pursued higher education and received technical honors within their engineering fields. One chose to become an entrepreneur. It has been extremely gratifying.

Anyone who is embarking on a new mentoring relationship should seek out individuals they deem as successful and ask them if they would consider being their mentor. As a mentee, you must be serious and committed to the work so that you don't waste your mentor's time. Typically, you want to find someone who is in leadership and progressing in their career who has either caught your eye or has been recommended to you. One of the biggest challenges I have experienced as a mentor is reaching out to someone, beginning to give them help, and then seeing them get to a point where they really aren't listening or taking my input to heart any longer. I've had to decide whether or not what I am doing is really helping that person, and if it isn't, I've chosen to step away and recommend someone else to continue as their mentor.

Having a sponsor is also crucial to success in today's professional environment. Most companies today are relational, meaning it is *who* you know rather than what you know that will get you in queue for opportunities for advancement. If you get into leadership circles where no one is advocating for you and people don't know you, others who are known and being advocated will get ahead of you. A sponsor should be someone who is well respected by their peers and is eager to bring up your name when opportunities arise. I was blessed with good sponsors who positioned me to soar. Mike MacKenzie was especially instrumental for me. It was through his persistent sponsorship that I went from starting off as a contributing engineer to becoming a director over a multibillion-dollar program. He advocated for me everywhere he went, and I went from a grade four to a grade seven status in just four years. That's a pace almost unheard of, but it was made possible because of his sponsorship.

―――――

When I'm not in the room, I want others to say that they appreciated my input as a mentor. It is that accomplishment—knowing that I have done something to help someone in their professional path, to make decisions, and advance—that makes me happy that I was able to give something back to their career. I am open to listen, available to teach, knowledgeable of my craft, and accountable to the success of mentees. That's my legacy as a mentor.

In the end, a mentor calibrates you for the knowledge that you need going forward, saying, "If you are going to be a well-rounded person, you need to not only be good at your technical skill and craft, but you also need to be technically sharp and confident in the politics of the company, the vision of the company, and how that aligns with you." The stages and phases along the way are all a part of the process—and it's a process I'm proud and blessed to have experienced and be a part of in people's lives.

Lonnie Goodson is an electrical engineer and a senior leader at a major defense contractor in Tucson, Arizona. He has over 30 years of professional experience in the defense, automotive, and primary metals industries. Lonnie has served progressively more significant leadership roles including program manager, deputy product line manager, and program director. He is also an active professional and personal mentor. Contact Lonnie at lgood6500@aol.com

6

Finding the Freedom

Terri Luna

I LIVE FOR the "aha" moment.

It happens when my clients discover they *do* have the answer to the opportunity they have brought to me. They see the origin of the challenge, understand what it is, and are willing to do whatever it takes to overcome it. It's a fabulous moment, is heartwarming and encouraging to me, and it brings a real sense of victory and freedom to my clients, even if they are not yet certain exactly how they are going to get across the finish line.

My role as a leadership and performance coach is to help people figure out why they have not been able to achieve something they want to accomplish, or to identify what is blocking them from being able to do what they want to do. I do this by asking what I call "empowering" questions, for which there are no "yes" or "no" responses, that challenge them to think about why they are struggling to find and implement a solution. This allows them to drill down to the cause of their adversity or to the energy behind their action or inaction. Once that is done, my job is to guide them to find the source of the issue by recognizing how things would be if they had already realized their goal. "What does that look like?" I want them to envision it, and as they do, they are freed to uncover the answer. I can then equip them to start creating an action plan to get where they want to be.

I'll never forget coaching Steve, an individual who found himself struggling to succeed in his well-paying job as a financial accountant specializing in mutual funds. While he had the knowledge and cognitive capacity to succeed, he began making uncharacteristic errors on spreadsheets like those that might have been made by someone who had just started the job, and he found himself frustrated in his current role. I had earlier shared with him that if we are not doing the thing that we really have a passion for doing, it can have a negative impact in the areas where we are trying to perform. So, I began to ask him empowering questions. "What do you find frustrating in your position?"

He replied, "I knew this job paid well, and I have a family. I have to provide."

When people use language like "I have to" or "I should," it's often a clue that they are not happy, and may even be shaming themselves, as if to say, "I just need to make this happen, no matter what." There was a lot going on with his family that made him think that he needed to do the accounting work, like it or not.

I then asked, "How can you see yourself improving your performance?" Steve didn't really have any good responses, which suggested he wasn't properly focusing on his work. That led me to inquire, "If you had your dream job, what would it be?" At that, Steve instantly responded that he

Finding the Freedom

had been thinking more and more about being a physical therapist, a far cry from being an accountant! I looked at him and said, "You do realize that the job that you are in is nowhere near where you want to be?" We chuckled, and then I asked, "How do you think you'll feel if you start taking steps towards being a physical therapist?" Steve acknowledged he'd feel less trapped in his current job, his energy levels would increase, and it would allow him to focus on excelling in *all* areas of his life. His new life would not seem so out of reach. That's freedom!

With that "aha" moment, Steve and I went to work to develop his plan to get to where he truly wanted to be, and not too long afterwards, he resigned. I never gave Steve the answers he needed. Our conversations allowed *him* to unveil the solutions he needed to move forward.

Today, Steve has not only accomplished his career goal, but he has overcome a near-death bout with cancer and has gone on to run multiple marathons established to provide funding to fight various forms of cancer.

There are some key distinctions between coaching and other ways to help people such as therapy, consulting, or mentoring. The difference between therapy and coaching is that a therapist helps their clients examine previous experiences that contribute to where they are today. It's more of a historical review to get the person to move beyond things that happened in the past that are creating dysfunctional behaviors in the present. A consultant is someone who is paid to use their knowledge and experience to tell their clients what to do. A coach, on the other hand, is not supposed to tell others what to do at all, but rather be that objective, non-judgmental voice to help them identify for themselves what they can do about a particular situation. While working with my clients I don't delve into their past experiences. As their coach I focus on moving my clients forward.

When it comes to mentoring, I intentionally strive to delineate between coaching and mentoring when I'm working with my clients. Part of the value of a mentor is to plant the seeds of suggestion into the mind of individuals, not by telling them what to do but by providing recommendations. As a coach, I avoid making suggestions so as not to unduly inform my client's answers with my opinions. I want them to come up with the answers they need on their own. As I compare coaching to mentoring, I honestly cannot think of a situation where I'm in coaching mode and transition into mentoring. It can definitely happen the other way around, though. Mentors may switch into coaching mode, and they should if they are equipped to do so and if they find their mentee has coachable barriers preventing them from reaching their goal.

While it is true that mentoring and coaching are distinct, the duo can be a great partnership for someone who is looking to advance in a particular organization or field. I see a mentor as being very helpful in that regard. As a leader, I have mentored people about their career and things they could consider as they progress. I have also mentored people when they had questions on how to address leadership or how to resolve issues. Coaching can come alongside a mentor to help a person overcome some innate challenges. Let's say they are not comfortable speaking in front of a crowd, so they don't participate in a meeting setting like they could.

Finding the Freedom

A mentor may help that person acknowledge that there are things they need to do to get themselves recognized in those meetings, and then a coach can come in and help that person uncover why they have a challenge speaking in front of others so they can overcome that hurdle.

One of my recent clients was being mentored at her job to improve communication with a fellow employee. The person was a peer, and my client was struggling because she didn't approve of the way this person did things. She was being mentored to develop a stronger bond with that individual. A situation came up where another person on the team also had a challenge with that same coworker. My client came to me and said, "I know I shouldn't get drawn into this situation between the two of them, but I am because I don't like the way he does things." As a coach, I asked her, "What do you want to do?" "What do you want to happen?" "What does success in this situation look like to you?" She responded, "I want to be able to tell the other coworker, 'You deal with him. I am not getting involved.'" I coached her to be able to do just that. Yet her mentor still had more work to do with her because she was not complying with what needed to be done to build a relationship with that individual. The ongoing value of mentoring is different from that of coaching, but they can work together well.

When I retired in 2018, I initially thought I'd go into consulting in a change management role. That is something that is called for everywhere and at all times, and it's largely what I did throughout my 30-plus-year career in the corporate world. But I knew I wanted to do something else, so I asked myself, "What do I *really* enjoy?" I thought about coaching because I did a lot of that with my co-workers and peers, believed I added value to people when I did, and really enjoyed seeing them get over their hurdles. I did some research on the proven impact of coaching, decided it was something I wanted to pursue, and got my certification.

When I coach, I often put on the change management hat that I used to wear as I helped teams get acclimated to technology or work design changes. Whenever a change needs to occur, I discovered that if the teams are engaged in every aspect of it, from the creation of it to the final implementation, they are far more accepting of the process. The same principle applies to coaching individuals. The client has a desired outcome, and I am there to help them fully engage the challenge they face and take ownership of it. In addition, as a coach, I find that I am both teacher and student. I have the opportunity to learn from each and every one of my clients in a nonjudgmental and objective way. It is just a matter of me listening to them, remaining curious about them, and helping them understand where they are and where they want to be. My role as a coach is to not get in that place with them, but to stay on the outside to help them through the process. In doing so, I get to enhance my listening skills, hearing things in an intuitive fashion so that I can listen for what they are *not* saying as much as to what they are.

I value *having* a coach as well because, as with everyone I coach, there are times when I want to accomplish some things and need to figure out why I am not. There was a point in my corporate career when I allowed myself to be rotated to various positions. It was done to enhance my exposure to different areas in the organization. Some of the moves were lateral; others were promotions. I loved learning new things, so it kept me engaged, and there were a lot of benefits to it. After 15 years of working these various roles, I realized I was feeling like a jack of all trades and a master of none. My energy was waning, and I found myself losing confidence in what I was bringing to the table. In hindsight, I know I could've used a coach at that time, but I didn't seek one because I was very independent. I worked well with teams, but when it came to addressing personal challenges, I felt like I had full ownership of that responsibility. I didn't think I needed the help. I had a mentor who was helping me navigate through some things, but mentorship alone was not addressing the internal feelings I had about myself. A coach, using the approach I now use, would've uncovered those feelings so I could've addressed them.

Reluctance to ask for help is the largest roadblock standing in the way of people engaging with a coach or mentor. People have misconceptions about both, and I know that when some hear the term "coach," they think of it as a real soft skill. That's why I usually don't say that I am a coach when I first engage with clients. Instead, I tell them that I help people accomplish the things that they find themselves struggling to achieve. Then the conversation leads to what that is, and I'll ask the person to think of something that they really want to do and how confident they are that they will actually get it done. If that person were to doubtfully reply, "I would *love* to retire in five years," I'd then ask why they don't think they can do that, and we'd talk about it. Perhaps they'll counter, "Well, you aren't supposed to retire when you are 55. You are supposed to retire when you are 67." I'd then ask why they believe that. Doing so uncovers how they feel about work, about being a provider for their family, and about the choices they can consider today to help them reach their goal. I'll ask what their passion is and whether or not they are working within that passion. All of this helps them begin to think outside of the box and consider other options.

As I've worked with my clients, I've discovered that the barriers people face to becoming successful can be both external and internal. For example, one person told me she wanted to launch her own business, but that she didn't have the capital to do so. The perceived lack of money was the external barrier. She then went on to reveal her internal reluctance to ask others for support. Another client told me he didn't see any value in networking with peers. "People are just phonies," he said, revealing the internal barrier. Then there are those who are simply afraid to step out of their comfort zones for whatever reason. Perhaps they have been in a secure position for many years. "Why not just ride it out?" they ask, fearful of external factors such as fluctuations in the economy. There are all kinds of external barriers that become internal because they keep people from doing what they love to do and could be successful doing. There are even those who feel guilty pursuing their goals and dreams because they feel like their family is going to have to somehow negatively bear the weight of that decision.

Another vital piece of effective coaching is helping people to identify their values and put them on paper. Those values should drive their actions or inactions, and I need to coach to those values. One person I worked with was an IT person who was making good money, and one of his values was being a provider for his family. Problem was, he wasn't happy as an IT person; in fact, he desired to open an art gallery.

Finding the Freedom

I helped him acknowledge and respect the value, but also to realize that if his job leaves him mentally or emotionally drained, bringing that negative energy home into his family's space could be affecting them in ways he was not yet seeing. That didn't mean he had to quit his IT job one day and open a gallery the next, but it did mean he had to acknowledge how his emotions were impacting others. He had competing values. He wanted to be a provider and emotionally sound for his family, but he was worn out and unhappy in his current situation. My goal is to facilitate self-realization and then have that person act on that realization.

When the client understands this, it's time to take action. We determine the goal, how likely it is to achieve, and place some measures around it. The SMART goal approach (specific, measurable, achievable, relevant, and time-based) is always good, and as a coach, we talk through all the goals and timeframes, with the client going back and working through their plan as needed to ensure they remain attainable.

I come from a small, very close-knit family. My parents, Emanuel and Janice, instilled the importance of education, saying that my sister, Merrie, and I were responsible for doing the work required to be successful. They were home every night and homework had to be done, but my parents never said, "Go do your homework." We knew we had to do it. While they provided guidance for us, they also expected us to independently think things through, using our logic to "figure it out" when it came to making decisions. That went a long way to inform what I am doing now as a mentor, coach, and consultant. I always valued the way they raised us. We'd ask them a question about doing something, and they'd ask, "What do you think about it?" We'd have to tell them, and by doing so, we got to see the consequences of our choices.

As a young teen, I was also fortunate to have teachers who mentored me, providing the guidance I needed to prepare me for my undergraduate studies and beyond. It was through their counsel and direction that I was well prepared to enter my collegiate years. The teacher who influenced me the most was Joyce Edwards, my seventh-grade English teacher. She was an African American woman from the south with that southern calm but firm demeanor. From a disciplinary standpoint, me and my fellow students knew we didn't want her to have to discipline us, nor did we ever want to disappoint her. She introduced me and others to the arts, including Alvin Ailey's dance troupe. We went to see them, and I remember the impact it had on everyone. Mrs. Edwards allowed us to be creative, and we did a lot of fun things together while at the same time learning about how to grow up with one another and how to help each other.

By the time I went to high school, I knew I was on the advanced placement path. I didn't have to figure that out. I wanted to go to college—after joining the U.S. Air Force first. My dad was totally against it. All my life he never really told me "yes" or "no" about anything, but all of a sudden it was, "No, I don't think you should do that." I was underage, still 17, and I needed their approval, and I would not consider going against their wishes. Following his "no," he counseled me, "You don't have the demeanor to be disciplined like you would have to be in the military. That's not the way you are." As I got older, I realized he was right. My home life and educational

Finding the Freedom

background had not prepared me for the discipline required to succeed in the military at that age. My dad knew my personality well enough to advise me, as a consultant would, about why the military was not a right fit for me.

As I reached young adulthood and entered into my profession, I recognized the immense value in having a mentor, someone to help me navigate my career. My first manager helped me understand the nuances and potential impacts of organizational redesigns. That knowledge informed my decision to later pursue a master's degree in organizational psychology and leadership and spend 15 years of my career in a change management capacity. Later in my career, I had mentors who helped me consider various job opportunities beyond the role itself, recognizing how important it was to reflect on how a job fit into my overall career strategy. It was during this time, along with hindsight, that I recognized the value of having both a mentor and a coach to work through external and internal challenges.

Considering what I, and many others, have gained from mentors and coaches, we should all be encouraged to provide the same support to others in need and share our lessons learned in life. In this way, we can pass on knowledge to help someone potentially avoid some of the pitfalls we encountered and possibly expedite their growth in their profession or life in general. It can be said that in every encounter with another, we have the opportunity to be both teacher and student. If we allow ourselves to be open and vulnerable enough not to bring pride or arrogance that can keep us from hearing what others say, then we have the opportunity to learn. We can think we are the teacher, the one bringing the knowledge. But if we listen to all of what someone else is sharing, we can learn a lot about them and ourselves. That brings freedom. We don't have to come into an engagement thinking we have all the answers or are responsible for making sure they do something right or wrong. We just need to be present enough and open enough so that we both walk away having learned and taught something.

Allow yourself this freedom—and you will find purpose and joy as you coach or mentor those around you.

Terri Luna is founder of 3T Luna Consulting, LLC, focusing on leadership and performance coaching, and previously served in various leadership positions for Vanguard. She now pursues her passion to provide coaching to individuals, teams, and organizations seeking to identify and overcome blocks preventing their optimal performance. Terri holds a bachelor's degree in Business Administration from the University of Pittsburgh and a master's degree in Organizational Psychology and Leadership from St. Joseph's University. Terri obtained her coaching certification from the Institute for Professional Excellence in Coaching (iPEC)©.

7

Come Into Your Own

Rosalind Longmire

BEING A SUCCESSFUL businessperson in my hometown of Tucson, Arizona for 18 years before being called into Christian ministry as a pastor at the church where I grew up may not seem like the typical career path.

But I'm blessed to say it was mine, and it was made possible, in part, through the mentors who came into my life along the way—mentors who have also equipped me to be an effective mentor to nurture, guide, and be a role model to others and help them come into their own.

I certainly had strong childhood examples that gave me a solid foundation to build upon. My maternal grandmother, Lena Brown, lived with us and took care of me and my two older sisters, Delma and Marva, while my parents were at work. My mother, Charsie, was a cook and maid for multiple families in northwest Tucson, while Nathaniel, my father, fulfilled a high-security role at Hughes Aircraft Company. They also owned and worked a janitorial business together at night.

The Purpose and Power of Mentorship

Being raised by my Grandmother Lena nurtured a great deal of wisdom in my life. It was her who first taught me to always be myself. She said people would notice me for who I was, not for who I tried to be.

In general, I was a shy kid who mostly kept to myself. I was a good student, but I didn't have a lot of friends throughout elementary and middle school because everyone saw me as being a "holy roller." I wasn't out late at night playing or getting into trouble. I also wasn't interested in some of the things they were doing. Despite the teasing, I tried to do the right thing and be kind because that's what I was taught to do. As I began high school, I was beginning to come into my own—though I didn't fully know what "my own" was quite yet. I had to get ready for the real world.

That was when I met my first mentor, track coach Marisella Kitt, and she was inspirational to me. In my freshman year, I was so timid that I did not want to get in the shower with the other girls for gym class. I got an F in Physical Education because I wouldn't dress out and participate. Then Coach Kitt arrived at the school, met with me, and asked how I got an F in PE. I told her, and she said, "Oh my goodness! I've watched you in the gym doing gymnastics and running. You have athletic abilities, and I think you would be good on the track team."

With her encouragement, I joined that squad my sophomore year, and once I started competing, I discovered that Coach Kitt was right. There was something inside of me that knew what she was saying was true. I liked to run. I could do that and do it well. She also told me, "There is something in you that is not like the other girls." She saw that I wasn't the typical rebellious teenager, even if I thought I was being rebellious because I wanted to fit in with the girls who went out smoking or were into boys when I wasn't. I wasn't sassy or disrespectful to her, either. Coach Kitt nurtured me in a different direction, saying that I had my own talents, abilities, and skills that made me who I was. Part of that was running track, so she spoke to the athlete and determined competitor inside of me. Mentors often see things in us that we don't see ourselves and try to pull it out. That is what she did with me.

Coach Kitt told me to keep my head up high and believe in myself, which helped me feel better about myself. With her influence, I came out of my shell. A lot of times the track team didn't come in first place, but we were always placed second or third from the other high schools in the city. I remember being proud of that. I really enjoyed it, and it helped to build my self-esteem.

Because of Coach Kitt's influence, I got involved in DECA, which still exists today to prepare emerging leaders and entrepreneurs for careers in marketing, finance, hospitality, and management in high schools and colleges around the globe. Even after I quit track to focus on that, Coach Kitt continued to have a positive effect on my desire to be in DECA and my emerging belief that I was going to be a businesswoman. She brought out the realization that I could accomplish something that is uniquely *me*, not by trying to be like everyone else, but just by being myself, exactly as Grandmother Lena had first taught me. I had the ability to decide what that was and what I wanted to be.

The Purpose and Power of Mentorship

Upon graduation from high school in 1977, I attended Pima Community College to earn an associate's degree in business administration. I didn't get my degree until 1993, though, because I worked and went to beauty school in between. In fact, I held a variety of jobs, from retail to manufacturing to office administration, before heading off to Allure Beauty College in the early 1980's. Once I earned my license from the Arizona State Board of Cosmetology, I worked as an apprentice for the person who became my second mentor, Doretta Scales. She was my personal hairstylist, and right before I decided to go to beauty school, Doretta was preparing to open her own salon. The business partner she was going to open the salon with moved away unexpectedly, and Doretta needed someone to help her set up the business. She knew from my family background that I was trustworthy, and I think she saw that in me. She also believed I'd be a hard worker and that I had some business skills. She asked if I needed a job, and I started doing those things for her.

Later, when I finished at Allure, I became Doretta's assistant in the salon. She mentored me by watching me and giving me tips about doing hair and relating to clients. She said our clients were our first priority. As I learned and practiced that, I quickly discovered that I enjoyed cosmetology because I loved talking to people and making them feel better about themselves. I found out I was a good listener, and Doretta helped me to value that as well. She was such a giving person, too, so she taught me how to treat people well and with respect.

During that time, I also met the man who would eventually become my husband at the barber shop where I went to get my eyebrows done. Al was 19 years older than me, but he was easy to talk to, a good listener, and a nice man. Pleasant, mild mannered, and low key, it was at the barber shop where I really got to know him better. We dated on and off for about 10 years before we got married. He, like Doretta, was client-oriented in his business. It wasn't really about money with either of them. It was about people—and because I loved people, it all naturally fit together for me. Doretta taught me the importance of relationships, and as I developed those relationships, I saw that cosmetology was as much about relationships as it was about beauty. I also ended up starting a relationship with Al that has become a lifelong one.

Before Doretta got married, we closed our shop, and I went to work for a few other salons before Al and I went into business together with a combo barber shop/beauty salon. By then, we had already been married for about three years. The shop was called Al's Barber Shop and Hair by Roz. A lot of Doretta's clients became my clients. That she would turn her clients over to me with full confidence that I could take care of them was very affirming.

I'm still an independent contractor today as a cosmetologist, working about 20-25 hours over three days each week. I don't work on Saturdays, though, because I now use that time to prepare for my sermons as a pastor at my childhood church, Phillip Chapel CME Church. I felt the call from God into the ministry in 2005. Three years after I was ordained, I went to work under my pastor, serving with her for two years before becoming pastor of Phillips Chapel in 2010.

The Purpose and Power of Mentorship

Today, I am known as "the pastor of love." My very first sermon, from John 4, was based on love.

Both Coach Kitt and Doretta influenced and informed the mentoring I do as a pastor through their encouragement of me. As a pastor, you encourage people. Because they did that for me, it made me want to do that for someone else. When somebody pours into you like that, you receive that and want to give it back. I recall the joy I felt mentoring one gentleman in my church on how to teach, nurturing that ability and helping him with self-discipline. He eventually started a study group for men, and he was able to relate to them, talk, and listen to them. At some level, he recognized he had leadership capability, but for whatever reason, he hadn't invested in that and drawn it out. I helped him see the leader inside himself, develop it, grow it, and use it. In the end, all teachers have to be leaders, regardless of whether they are teaching a child in Sunday School or an adult in a small group study.

I also had the privilege of mentoring a young woman on how to be a good mother. That natural instinct to be one was already in her. I had seen it in her before she had her daughter. But she was telling herself that she couldn't be a good mother. That was in her head, probably fed by her circumstances. I helped her take more time with her child to teach her and train her up in a way that she could develop into a healthy child that knew that she was loved. The young woman didn't really have that to draw from in her life, so she needed to know she could do it.

I believe there are just some things we don't know on our own. Even if we believe we can do it and want to be our own person, we always need someone to encourage us or pull on our coattails if we are going in the wrong direction. We need someone there to instruct us, and because of their experiences, give us a little heads up so it's not so hard. That, to me, is the voice of a mentor.

Every one of us is purposed to give back something. Whether it is time, influence, or experience, open yourself up to help somebody along the way. We are all here to encourage one another. I believe anyone who has been mentored before has that and wants to do that. It is an essential part of our human nature. I had a young man come up to me that I hadn't seen in quite a while. He had worked in the barber shop sweeping up hair. He said, "Thank you for always being so nice and encouraging to me."

To have him say that reminded me that even the little things we do to pour into people are the greatest things that we can possibly do—and will help them come into their own.

Rosalind Longmire is pastor of Phillips Chapel CME Church, the church where she has served all of her life, and she is also a licensed cosmetologist. Her heart's desire is to allow God to use her to build His Kingdom through loving, serving others, teaching, and preaching the Gospel of Jesus Christ. Contact Rosalind at rozlong52@aol.com

8

Moments of Impact

Marvin Carolina Jr.

I AM AN A-B-C, 1-2-3 kind of guy. I always have been. That has been my approach from my upbringing, through my pursuit of an industrial management degree at the Georgia Institute of Technology, and into my early career in sales and leadership at Oscar Mayer and Kraft Foods, Carolina Beverage Distributing, and Sears. It continued during my 25 years of service as vice president of diversity at J.E. Dunn Construction. It remains my approach today as president and CEO of the Better Business Bureau of Greater Kansas City and in my work as a public speaker, trainer, and consultant.

I like to keep things basic—so, when it comes to mentorship, I believe it is all about people. Whether I'm a mentor, a mentee, or whatever the categorization, I just want to help others succeed.

In many ways, mentorship begins in our lives as we observe people. No one is necessarily telling us, "You have to do this." We watch others, and we mimic their behavior. My father, Marvin, Sr., and my grandfather, Charles, were not very talkative people. Both of them were pretty laid-back guys. But they led by example. Their behavior demonstrated it. When I was a kid, my mother, Jeannette, would drop me off to hang around with my grandfather. He was retired, and throughout the day we'd drive around, pick up friends from church or elsewhere, and take them to doctor's appointments or to the grocery store. I saw how he'd get out of the car, open their door, and let them go in. He'd always ask, "Do you want me to come in with you, or are you okay?" After a while, I started doing the same thing, jumping out of the car and running around to see if they wanted me to come in with them. That's where my desire to help others started.

My father was also a deacon at a church. We used to drive around as he gave love offerings to people in our church, New Hope Baptist Church, each year over the Christmas holiday. During my freshman year in college, I came home for winter break, and I was down and out. I was on a full athletic scholarship, but the semester had been bad academically. I wasn't even sure then that I'd be able to keep the scholarship, much less stay on the team. My attitude was lousy. Then dad asked me to join him as he made the rounds to hand out the love offerings. We first visited a home where the woman was bedridden. Her granddaughter met us at the door. She was upbeat. "Today's a good day," she said, referring to the woman, "because she is talkative and doing things." We prayed for her as we left the offering. At the next house, the man we visited was unemployed. As we gave him a gift basket, he called out to me, smiling, "Hey, how's that football? Are you showing them how to play down there in Georgia?"

Those people were in tough situations, but they were all in great spirits when we stopped by. They were happy to see me; it was a great time—and my father never said a word. He could've said, "Did you learn from that?" But he didn't have to. All he did was thank me for riding with him. My father's actions that day taught me that it is not all about me. Helping others was all that mattered. I had nothing to complain about, and I needed to be happy right where I was.

I also learned about caring for others, and being cared for, from my high school coach, Bob Grandizio. I went to a private high school that was also a boarding school where I'd live during the week, going home only on the weekends. It was a tremendous change for me my freshman year, and I called home often because I was so homesick. I was so upset I also struggled in my classes. Coach Grandizio always checked up on me, and at one point, my dorm room was moved so that it was close to where he lived. I never found out if that was done intentionally, but he stopped by often, asking about my classes and making sure nothing was wrong. I was ready to leave that school. I didn't think it was going to work for me. But Coach Grandizio made all the difference for me that first year.

Those examples, and the foundation they laid in my life, drives my commitment to help entrepreneurs, executives, and business owners. It also fuels my desire to mentor others to reach their dream of owning their own business. I share my experiences in corporate marketing and business development with them, and I relate what I learned when I returned to school to get a master's degree in community development from North Park University. I help people get to the next level using my resources and knowledge base, and I love doing it.

I've noticed that Baby Boomers like me are passing on their knowledge to Millennials more than ever, and the younger generation welcomes this. While mentorship is typically done from an older to younger person, it can happen with any generation reaching out to any generation. I can absolutely be mentored by someone younger than me. It's all about the knowledge base being shared.

Just since 2019, I've had four different people come up to me and ask to be mentored. I've mentored people here and there over the years, but to have four successful people ask in such a short period of time has never happened to me before. Different people referred them to me, and each one has been a tremendous experience. They've listened. They've shown up on time and come prepared. Each one had some serious things come up in their life that required some serious decision making. I gave them specific things to consider, they went home and thought about it, and then came back the next week so we could work through more issues. One received an offer from another company, and he included me in that process. Another was looking for a different job and needed advice. Yet another was looking to make some moves within the organization he worked for and sought my insights. The fourth was a childhood friend I hadn't spoken to in years that connected with me on social media. She asked if I'd be willing to talk to her son who had just graduated from college. She wanted him to receive direction from me about where to go next and how to go about it.

In addition to these, there was a high school student named Chris who was an intern at my office. When I told him he needed to wear a shirt and tie, he told me he only had one shirt and didn't own any ties. The next day, I brought in a handful of ties for him to wear, and then took him out and bought him some shirts. My involvement caused Chris to start coming into my office during his lunch break to talk, and he asked me questions about a lot of different things. Our relationship developed, and during his senior year, I asked him what college he was planning to attend.

"I haven't considered college," he replied.

"But this is an internship for college bound students," I said. "You need to go to college."

He began looking at schools. He continued interning during his freshman and sophomore years of college, and eventually, he found a job with a major car rental agency. He ended up working there for several years. "I never had any idea to go to college," Chris later shared with me.

I supported Chris, helped him along the way, and tried to be a living example for him. Today, he has a degree, a wonderful career, a wife, and a home.

I was just out of college from the Georgia Institute of Technology when formal mentorship had the first major impact on me. I went to work for Oscar Mayer in Portland, OR, and I didn't know anyone there. One of the people I worked with, Dan, took me under his wing and showed me what I needed to do to be successful. He really helped me to understand the corporate structure and the processes and procedures of the company from a sales perspective. He often asked me to meet him for breakfast or lunch, and sometimes invited me to dinner with his family since I didn't have any family in Portland. I recall one time when I messed up the pudding snack displays in three different grocery stores and the senior vice president of one of the stores yelled at him about it. Dan came down hard on me. I fixed the problem, and we moved forward. But I often use that story today as an example of how I could have crumbled. I could have been upset at him and disappointed in myself—but I wasn't because I knew that while his actions may not have been ideal, he was trying to help me. It was tough love.

When I reconnected with Dan years later and told him that story, he shared he had always felt bad about how he responded. I reminded him of how he had helped me acclimate from college to the realities of corporate America, and I emphasized that it was a really good experience for me.

Another formal mentor in my life was Ricky. Back when I was rolling out a small business development program, he not only told me I had a special program, but that he appreciated the passion and compassion with which I delivered it. Just the way he said that had a great impact on me. It meant a lot. Since then, Ricky has supported me in many different ways. Every time I go to where he works and lives in Atlanta, we have dinner. Each time, he has given me some really nice nuggets: things I am doing, things I should be doing, and things I can do differently.

There are three basic aspects to helping people that I use as I mentor others: trust, respect, and best interest. It starts with me doing everything I can so that the other person is able to trust that I believe in what I am saying to them, and that I have the skill level to help them. Much of that comes down to really knowing what you are saying. Do your background and credentials position you to truly help them? When that's established, they will then respect you and what you are sharing with them. It is almost like when you tell your kids something and it works out that you were correct.

Moments of Impact

When I was a kid, I often thought, "Why did my parents have to be right about that?" It caused me to respect their opinion and ask for it more often, and that's how you want others to respond to you as a mentor. They see who you are, and the relationship grows.

Once trust is built and respect is earned, you then show that you are acting in their best interest. Others can tell that you are genuine, making the extra effort, and that it is not about you. You want them to see the proof of what you are doing for them. When I was a young guy in my twenties working for Oscar Mayer, I lived in San Diego, CA and started coaching a basketball team at the YMCA as a volunteer. I was an athletic guy, had played football in college, and I enjoyed basketball. Each week, I discovered that the kids came and went. Sometimes only three players showed up, and we didn't have enough to practice; other times, we had enough attend to place two full teams on the court. Either way, I coached them the same exact way. I worked with them as if they were in the National Basketball Association. No matter who was there, they saw I was invested in them. At one point, I rented a van so we could make a trip up the coast to Los Angeles to go to Magic Mountain.

When they showed up, they looked at the van and asked, "Coach? Why didn't you just use the van the Y has?"

I said, "I don't work for the Y."

"So how did you get this van if you don't work for the Y?"

"I rented it."

"With your money?"

"Yeah."

"Why?"

"Because we are having a good time."

My commitment to the team had already escalated, and they knew that—but when they understood what I had done, *their* commitment rose to a different level. They saw I was spending my money to do something for them. I also bought the tickets to get inside the amusement park. It changed everything.

Adults see this, too. When someone asks to meet with me, they'll sometimes say, "I don't want to take up too much of your time." I tell them to sit down, and I cross my legs to show that I'm not in a hurry. "Do you want to talk?" I say. "Let's continue to talk." That's when they understand that I have their best interest in mind. Years later, they'll say, "I remember the first time I met with you. You didn't rush me out. You didn't ask me some quick questions to get me out the door. You acted like you had a lot of time, and you let me sit there and talk. You didn't talk over me, either." It reminded me again how we shape people's lives by our behavior—just as my father and grandfather did with me.

As I sit here on the back side of life—the back nine, rounding third base, the home stretch—I reflect on my journey, the people who have helped me, and, subsequently, the people who I have helped. We call it mentoring, coaching, or sponsorship, but being a simple person, I just call it helping others. As I have become older, I have become very intentional in the way that I help and assist people. How I mentor, coach, and sponsor is much more structured and detailed than ever before. I give homework and research projects, ask uncomfortable questions, and give uncomfortable tasks because we grow through discomfort, reaching beyond what we thought was possible.

Still, as I flashback over my lifetime and think of all the people who have coached, mentored, sponsored, or just plain helped me, I see that the vast majority of it was unstructured with little detail. Most of all, it was unconscious. Whether that help came from my parents, relatives, sports coaches, family friends, business colleagues, or even strangers, it went beyond gender, ethnicity, and age.

When I close my eyes and look back at these moments, they make me smile, laugh, and even get a little emotional. Some moments lasted just a day; others occurred over weeks, months, or years—but the impact of these moments has lasted a lifetime.

May we all play a role in bettering the lives of those around us. By the way we live, we can create moments of impact and help others reach their dreams.

Marvin Carolina Jr. serves as president and CEO of the Better Business Bureau of Greater Kansas City. He is also a trainer, a consultant, a member of the National Speakers Association, and the author of two books focused on entrepreneurship and small businesses, *Across the Middle: Entrepreneur for Growth and Success*, and *Build to Win: A Playbook for Entrepreneurial Success*. Contact Marvin at marvin@kansascity.bbb.org

9

Give Back

Dr. Amanda H. Goodson

WHENEVER PEOPLE ASK me about mentoring, I encourage them to get a "Seven Up!"

No, I don't mean the lemon-lime soft drink still known as "The Uncola." For me, the term "Seven Up" refers instead to the number of mentors or coaches I recommend anyone should have at any one time.

I know, that may sound like a lot. But because I believe mentorship is critical in every area—business, industry, academia, at a not-for-profit organization, even for a volunteer—the amount is more than justified. In fact, the very success of people and teams hinge on mentorship. I can tell a well-organized individual or a well-oiled team by the mentorship they've received.

In all our roles in life, we should have someone who can help us along the way early and often. It's nurturing. It's essential—and it's something I have the privilege of providing (using my Unlock Your Full Potential and Goodson 9 Block / FRESH WILL programs) as well as receiving from a variety of personal and professional mentors who comprise my refreshing "Seven Up."

A mentor is many things. He or she is someone who has gone somewhere we want to be and has done it successfully over and over again. It is someone who is two, three, or even four levels ahead of where we are in our different areas of expertise. A mentor is someone who has a diverse, deep portfolio that can aid us in a number of categories. It is a person who sees something amazing in us and is eager to equip us to do something we never thought we could achieve. A mentor is a futurist—someone who helps us with strategy and causes us to think 10 or even 20 years ahead of where we are so that we can develop a plan and a platform to get us there. If we are with someone who is at the same level, or even one level ahead, that person certainly has value. But he or she is not a strategic mentor.

With our "Seven Up" set of mentors in place, we'll move quicker, attain high performance, and be highly valued contributors in any setting. High-performance people help with the cadence and rhythm of how an organization is breathing and moving. Highly valued people are seen as the top of the heap and bring with them an expectation of reaching new levels of leadership. Mentorship allows us to discern and see the differences between the two. Mentors also teach us how to be leaders. This includes branding, our executive presence, the shaping of our vernacular, and how we make transactions of our wealth of knowledge with other leaders. Mentorship impacts how we interact with others and "show up" in a room. Mentorship informs how we want to be remembered, and it allows us to improve our thought processes as we develop the neurolinguistics (the fundamental dynamics between mind [neuro] and language [linguistic]) of our leadership presence and execution.

Mentorship is especially vital in enabling us to know and leverage the culture we encounter, particularly in an academia setting where the vernacular we use is paramount, or in a business environment where a certain savvy, an executive presence, is required. In business, a specific rhythm and cadence is expected. It is about performance, making money, and more money. In a not-for-profit, meeting the vision and the mission of the organization is most important. They want money, too, but the methodology is different, and our performance has to be more relational, collaborative, and supportive.

A mentor who understands the cultures of these varied settings and has been in that culture for a while is priceless. Management consultant, educator, and writer Peter Drucker rightly stated, "Culture will eat strategy for lunch." A mentor that understands culture helps us to be in alignment with what is going on so we can make the right decisions. When systems engineer Abraham (his nickname is A.B.) moved from Mississippi to become one of my coworkers at a major defense contractor in Arizona, he had to adjust from the general culture of the deep south to the one that exists in the southwestern U.S. He also had to get used to an entirely different work culture. He took on a number of mentors to help him learn the hierarchy of organization in our more military-focused culture and to understand the type of work we do and how it benefits the nation. We made ourselves available to him as much as possible. Through the mentoring, A.B. was equipped to develop a strategy to be successful. He embraced it so well that he placed himself on an accelerated path as a high-performing engineer. He took the mentoring seriously. He didn't buck against the system, and it helped. The better you understand culture and how you, your strategies, and goals fit into it, without compromising who you are, the better off you will be.

Je're provides one of my most successful mentoring stories away from my workplace. She was a really good student in high school and went off to college to major in engineering. But she found the classes to be different and harder than what she experienced in high school. It was also overwhelming to her being at such a big university and being away from her family back home. Before long, she left school and returned home, but she wasn't dejected. She was proactive and worked several odd jobs before ending up at a company specializing in inventory for retailers. She travelled to stores throughout her city and surrounding communities, establishing such an excellent reputation that she became a supervisor overseeing a team of people. Je're found the job to be satisfying, and she thought she was successful because she was a supervisor.

When I began mentoring her, we had a conversation about where she wanted to go next. We agreed that she would never get the benefits of a full-time employee such as a 401(k) staying where she was. She also didn't have a plan of action for later on in life, and we went to work on that together.

As she started applying for other jobs, I encouraged Je're to visualize in her mind what she wanted to do and what kind of job she wanted to have. I directed her to write a letter to herself stating the goals for the type of job she desired. Guess what happened? She ended up getting a job at a major U.S. defense contractor in security—and she loved it! She's had two or three promotions since then with merit pay increases to match. Now she has a 401(k) and is saving for her retirement. In addition, Je're returned to school to finish her degree.

I was humbled and excited as I saw how my mentorship allowed Je're to think outside of the box. She identified solutions to her problems that she never thought about before. As we continue to work together, I see the potential within her. I see what motivates her. I know how she thinks, and I discern the direction of her heart. I take all of that to help her solve problems and create new opportunities. I don't recommend anything I don't think she can do. Je're says I sometimes push her hard, but I do that to show her the big beautiful package she can have if she just takes a couple of extra steps forward.

There are three characteristics all successful mentors share. First, they genuinely *care about their mentees* and want the best for them. They get to know them as a person, understanding their life goals and their expectations. These mentors ask for permission to provide honest and direct feedback, knowing that people will listen to them and respond positively when they know they are cared for. Secondly, mentors are *honest and brave,* but not "brutally" honest in such a way as to damage their mentees or their relationships with them. Instead, they keep the other person's interests foremost in their mind and demonstrate how their suggestions will help their mentees to be more successful and increase their ability to reach their goals. Finally, successful mentors *help others see their blind spots and grow.*

The Purpose and Power of Mentorship

It is likely they will need to tell their mentees something that many other people already know, but the mentee doesn't. Additionally, these mentors understand that growth often requires experiential learning, and they look for opportunities beyond their conversations. For example, a mentor might recommend a special work assignment, a volunteer opportunity, working with a specific expert, taking a class, or even teaching one. The right experience will help mentees learn that they usually can't think themselves into a new way of acting. Instead, they need to act themselves into a new way of thinking.

I'm blessed to have several mentors who exemplify these characteristics, covering areas from business, technical, and legal to financial and spiritual. After working on hardware throughout my engineering career, I was given responsibility over information technology before transitioning again into customer relationship management. My supervisor became Kevin Oxnam, and he was a Six Sigma Master Black Belt expert. As such, he looked at value with the eyes of a customer, and he determined how utmost value delivery could be created in a system that causes continuous improvement to emerge. Every time I saw Kevin, he'd always say, "Good morning!" He had a nice laugh, and he had character, integrity, and knowledge. I'd see Kevin go into a room and change the whole makeup of the place just through his presence. He'd sit, listen, and allow the team to brainstorm so we could do what we needed to do. He eloquently influenced us in ways we hadn't been before.

Kevin also mentored me professionally. Whenever I thought what I was doing was going in the wrong direction or didn't add the value it should, he corrected me, not by saying I was wrong, but by saying, "Let's think about it like this or like that." This built me up and raised my level of thinking and awareness. He introduced me to *The Goal*, a book by Eliyahu M. Goldratt and Jeff Cox, and he gave me other things to read to help me improve and reach higher heights as I applied the principles I learned.

My spiritual mentor, Dr. Laura Thompson, is especially effective in getting my thoughts and spirit in alignment with peace, love, my faith, and what I believe, while doing the things I need to do daily without encumbrances from emotional baggage and traumas. In relation to this, I am a certified DiSC trainer, and I use assessments, as a mentor, to help my clients identify their leadership type, their personality type, and how they manage teams. I coach as well, but there is a distinction between mentoring and coaching. Mentors go deep and help their clients within the framework of their craft, whereas a coach goes wide and high and sees a bigger terrain. I have coached clients in a variety of fields including government, business, not-for-profits, and website design. Valerie employed me as a workforce coach. She was looking to try to add better value to her organization as well as to be a better professional. We used a SPOT analysis to look at her professional vision from the standpoint of four key tests of her current workplace reality: strengths (S), potential areas for improvement (P), opportunities (O), and threats (T). Strengths represented areas where Valerie believed she was most effective and therefore placed her in a position of advantage. Her potential areas for improvement came from places where she felt she was at a disadvantage and therefore needed more training or development. Her opportunities constituted areas that she believed she could exploit to even greater advantage. Threats were elements, usually external, that could damage or even endanger her ability to fulfill her vision.

I encourage my clients to assess their strengths, potential areas for improvement, opportunities, and threats from any starting point with which they feel most comfortable. In our coaching, we identified Valerie's main strength as technical acumen. Her threat was collaboration because she worked with some people that she didn't feel she could trust enough to be able to do her work properly. We identified opportunities she could put out there on the table so that people could clearly see her technical acumen, and pinpointed potential areas for improvement that could remove the threat and help her be perceived by others as a professional partner. Valerie also dressed more casually than her colleagues, so I coached her on how she could change her appearance to exhibit a strong executive presence. Valerie took everything she learned, leveraged it, and ultimately accepted an offer from another company that increased her status and compensation.

In terms of sponsorship, I had a wonderful sponsor, Wiley Bunn, whose story is related in my book, *Astronomical Leadership* (along with my Input-Process-Output coaching process and Goodson 9 Block / FRESH WILL program). He had my name tattooed on his brain and on his heart. Whenever he went into a room knowing there was an opportunity, he always put my name on the table, saying, "She deserves a chance. She will be successful because you'll help her to be successful. I'll make sure she is successful." Inspired by Wiley and the amazing impact he had on my life, championing me to become the first African American woman to ever hold the position of Director

Give Back

of Safety and Mission Assurance at the National Aeronautics and Space Administration, I sponsor others as well.

My mother Mable's best friend was Bettye Dixie. She was a business coach, and there were times my parents took me over to her house when I was a young person. She always gave me a booster shot of advice and wisdom, helping me to think differently about how I spoke, how I acted, and how I navigated through challenges I faced. She consistently saw things in me that I didn't see. She told me stories with hypothetical situations and then asked what I thought of them. She told me it would be difficult for a young African American woman to be seen in a certain light, particularly in areas that were male dominated, and that I needed to be excellent for people to recognize me and my abilities. Bettye Dixie always made an impression on me. She was an early mentor when I didn't even realize I was being mentored, and one of the key people who helped me become who I am today.

The legacy I want to leave as a mentor is for my mentees to know they were catapulted into a totally different realm and a completely different space because they followed the steps we worked on together. I want them to realize they followed the process, it worked, and it caused them to write an indelible impression in eternity. Evangelist, author, speaker, and leadership consultant Miles Munroe says we should "die empty." I strive to empty myself to a person by giving them the best that I have—and as I do, I get more knowledge. I get taller. I get stronger. I can help more and support more. The more I give, the more that is given back to me.

The Purpose and Power of Mentorship

Don't stop, and don't be discouraged when things are not going your way. Find a person or a group that can help you, and then let them know you appreciate them. I read a lot of books, and I've gone across the country to meet people who have mentored me through their books. All I wanted to do was shake their hand. I did that with Miles Munroe and others, like author and teacher Apostle John Eckhardt. In the end, I believe anything you need is available to you. It just takes a little research.

And, as you are looking for someone to mentor or coach you, to be your beacon or North Star, be that North Star for someone else as well. You have something in you that will create a compelling future for someone else.

No matter who you are, you've got something to give back.

Dr. Amanda H. Goodson is owner and founder of Amanda Goodson Global, LLC, and has over 25 years of experience supporting government agencies, corporate industry, and academia as a leadership strategist, professional coach and consultant, workshop facilitator, and keynote speaker for emerging, mid-level, and student/developing leaders as well as for churches and faith-based groups. She is a senior leader for a major defense contractor in Tucson, AZ, and pastor at Trinity Temple CME Church in Tucson. Contact Amanda at amandagoodsonglobal@gmail.com

10

Get in the Right Lane

Robert W. Merriweather

I LOOK AT mentoring a little differently than most—in that I do not really see it as a formal process. Perhaps that comes, in part, from the fact that I have been coached more than mentored, particularly in connection with my 34-plus year career with an American multinational package delivery and supply chain management company. The mentoring I received occurred as I was growing up in my hometown of Paducah, Kentucky and continued between school and church throughout my upbringing there. The mentoring focused on building my life skills, while coaching came later through my workplace.

There was not any one particular person who mentored me, but it was more of a collective of individuals who, at different times and various ways, poured their knowledge and insight into me. Adults at my church embraced me and my peers, making sure we had experiences that were good for us and challenged us to aspire to recreate those positive things within our church family. We were always given opportunities to do speeches, participate in the annual Christmas play and Easter pageant, and give lesson overviews to the group in Sunday School and during assemblies. Those experiences helped me to develop how I presented myself, spoke up, and became comfortable with public speaking.

In our small-town community, school was also quite valuable. My high school was diverse in population, yet we embraced each other, and our educators made sure we knew it was important for us to excel and do well. The value of diversity is learning how to get along and being able to accept one another for what each person brings to the table. We connected with the community through our extracurricular activities, sports, and academics. Many students from that high school went on to college, several on scholarships, and some went to the military.

While attending the University of Evansville in Indiana, I started my career part-time with the delivery and supply chain management company, where I moved up several different levels of management and leadership within the organization. After over three decades, I have learned a lot, through experiences, competencies acquired, successes, and challenges about how to interact with other leaders. I have also discovered how to create respect amongst peers, subordinates, and with those who I have reported to. The respect I have gained gets things done from a supported team perspective.

My coaching opportunities at the company came as I worked with people from every demographic in the United States. At the entry level, we are probably one of the few companies where someone can still come in and work their way up into a successful career, including one in management. Both managers and non-management people take time out with staff to coach and train them along the way. This involves working with others when they do something incorrectly to show them how to perform, creating accountability. It also includes conducting role play exercises with one another to practice actual situations that can arise with colleagues or customers to gain practical knowledge. This type of coaching is more hands-on, and it can occur with those you report to, people that report to you, and can even cross peer lines.

I recall early in my career when I had to make it as a driver, or else I was not going to have a job. I started as a part-time, hourly laborer, progressed into part-time management, and then left that role to take on the driving job as a step toward going into full-time management. This created some intense pressure, and I struggled at the beginning, but it was one of the union stewards who lived in my neighborhood who took the time to provide insights I needed to move forward. He taught me not to overthink the job, but to take it one step at a time. What he really pushed through to me was that each delivery comes through one at a time: line it up, get it off, then go on to the next section. It was all about breaking it down to the simplest process. After that interaction, my stress went down, and my productivity went way up. I was able to do really well on the job and accomplish my permanency as a driver. It was a pivotal moment where I discovered the importance of peer to-peer interaction. He cared enough to make sure I was successful.

———

"Get in the Right Lane" is the name of the process I use that focuses on the three areas of coaching, mentoring, and sponsoring. As a coach, these individuals usually report directly to me, or sometimes they are reporting to others. For example, there might be an employee with a performance problem in which basic supervision does not fully help the employee. My first step is to get to know and build trust with that person. Part of that includes sharing life experiences or circumstances so they can understand that they are not the only one that is going through what they are experiencing. I want them to know that I have been there, and so have others around them. They are not alone, and there is a solution to improve their results.

Mentoring occurs when I have spent time coaching a person and understand the goals they want to accomplish, either in life or in an area where I have some expertise in the company. I strive to give them tools so they can get to where they want, providing them the exposure to make sure they get the experience needed that fits their profile so they can attain their desired goals.

I put a little twist on sponsorship, in that, being in a pyramid-structured management company, we need people who can fill key positions and roles along the way. When working for a large corporation that is fast paced and requires being nimble, you must adapt quickly to change. I teach people how to sustain and maintain where they are so they can continue or, if the circumstance warrants, push that person along to a different role and speak up on their behalf.

When I am in direct contact with them, I spend more time coaching with management because they are in my purview. Those individuals can choose to stay in contact with me or allow me to mentor them once they are done with coaching. I usually mentor someone once I am no longer their direct manager. Sponsorship can come into play when a person is under my direct supervision or in situations where I can simply pick up the phone and support someone to help them overcome a struggle, work out a problem, or advance. I can reach out to their manager or give some guidance to that manager regarding the given situation. Sometimes it is best for the person to maintain their position and be successful where they are.

My "Coaching in the Current" process refers to coaching others in the flow of where they are at that given time. It starts by examining the opportunities in front of them and examining whether or not role play can contribute to their learning. Let's say a supervisor who has been doing a job for one year comes to me and says, "I have a driver that has been with the company for 30 years and knows his job inside out, but I have to talk to him about the amount of non-productive time during his day." I will role play with that supervisor to give them an opportunity to engage that employee effectively and improve their production.

Next, I try to constructively dissect what happened as a result of that interaction. "Well, the first hour I was with him," the supervisor responded, "he was not going to listen, debated the training given, and gave every reason and an excuse for not being able to perform as trained." We then talked about a time the supervisor struggled with being productive himself. "Yeah, I mentioned that," he said. "It opened up the conversation, and I was able to incorporate my real-life experiences." Then I close by helping the supervisor adjust for future interactions, affirming what he learned so he could have those tools in his communication toolbelt. With every new interaction, more useful tools are added to the belt. As a coach, I am mainly working to help the person be able to identify the issue, outline what they need to do, and move forward. I want to get them to where they can make the decisions on their own.

The Purpose and Power of Mentorship

In the process I call "Mentor to the Milestones," the first aspect is to learn the person's goals by getting to know them and allowing them to get to know me. My job is to learn what that person wants and what they seek out in a career. If I do not take the time to understand their career goals, I cannot give them the experiences they need to prepare them for the next level.

Next, I seek to guide them into an understanding of their true potential. I might mentor someone who is an outstanding one-on-one communicator but struggles with public speaking or setting up a video conference call. These are areas they have to improve upon and overcome. If they are not willing to put in the work on these development areas, they will become barriers to their advancement. Tough conversations will be required to help them see that their potential might be limited if they are not willing to change. It requires getting them to be honest with themselves, and that is not always easy. A lot of younger workers come in saying they are going to be CEO, and I have to help them understand that while everybody cannot be CEO, they can still be in leadership.

Once that is achieved, we can then mentor together to create a plan that will propel them toward their goals that involves exposure, including the sell. I work with a group of managers to make sure that person gets the exposure they need by rotating them into specific positions, tasks, or roles that are essential to meeting their career goals. It might not be in my operation, but a neighboring one, and that is okay. The reason I emphasize "including the sell" comes from one of the things my parents told me: "Always ask for what you want. All people can tell you is 'yes' or 'no.'" So many people miss out because they never really *ask* for what they want. At the end of the day, you have to be willing to speak up for yourself.

Get in the Right Lane

Finally, my "Sponsor to Sustain" approach begins with holding and thriving. Sometimes there will be those who can be outstanding or effective managers or supervisors, but through behavioral observation I am able to discern there are skills or characteristics they might not want to develop. I believe they might not be the best fit for the goal they are pursuing. I have seen people get promoted yet fail. I have seen others who become miserable after they achieve their desired position. So, as a sponsor, sometimes I need to say to a leader, "Hey, I had a conversation with this person, and they are happy where they are. They don't mind taking different assignments at the same level, but let's maintain them because they do the job that we expect." This requires honesty in assessing an individual, experience, and being sure to take the time to engage the person. There should be no surprises.

I worked with a young man who went from a bachelor's to a master's degree and wanted to get promoted accordingly. He was from a different country, and he had a heavy accent. I told him that people may not take the time to hear what he had to say because his accent made it hard for them to understand what he was saying. I suggested he take a class to help develop his vocal skills. He followed through, and he got promoted in the next 18 months. I was able to get the point across to him that others were not really going to listen to him if they could not understand what he was saying. It was an epiphany that prompted him to act, and he ultimately saw the reward for his efforts.

As you can probably tell, I do not see coaching, mentoring,

and sponsoring to be mutually exclusive. All three require an informal process and the wisdom to know where I am in that process with each individual. I do not have a set group of people for "Get in the Right Lane," but at any given time I am working with 10 to 12 different people. In addition, if I hear that a management person that I have worked with in the past is having a tough time, I will pick up the phone, call, and assess. Perhaps I can recommend someone in their management structure to speak to. Basically, if I say I am going to be there for someone, I am there. That is so important as a coach, mentor, or sponsor. I want to be there for people and make a difference. I will never forget the young lady who came in to work every day and did an outstanding job in her role but did not really know how to present herself as a leader. She had a bachelor's degree from an in-state university, but she was doing an entry level job. "You should be in full-time management," I counseled her, "where you can excel and move forward in your career." I got her to focus on becoming more professional in how she presented herself, and she excelled. It was all about helping her refocus and make slight changes that she had not put a lot of thought into because she didn't realize her own potential. She ultimately became a manager.

I also strive to be as available as I can for my friends or family members. I had a high school friend with whom I had maintained contact over the years. At one point, he was in-between jobs looking for an opportunity to do something different. I knew his background was in engineering, and I knew his work ethic. I asked him to send me his resume and his interests. "Did you want to stay in the engineering field?" I asked him. "Yes," he replied, "with focus on compliance and safety." I made a few contacts, and he was set up for an interview through human resources, and then another via an engineering group. That alone opened up multiple avenues for him to choose from. He was hired, and he has been a successful engineer for 20-plus years with the company.

People being there for you is priceless. One of my favorite sayings is, "Say what you mean, and mean what you say." It is a principle I value because I know how I have felt when someone was there for me. Reach out to someone for help and be willing to help others as well. There's no better way to make sure you get in the right lane and stay on course.

Robert W. Merriweather is a business manager with 30-plus years of management experience working for a multinational package delivery and supply chain management company. He has worked in operations, industrial engineering, and quality control, as well as process analysis, cost reduction/containment, safety compliance, labor relations, succession planning, and fundraising. Robert is founder of the Constance D. Merriweather Scholarship Fund, one of the avenues he uses to give back which he considers to be one of his most honorable accomplishments. Contact Robert at rwmerriweather@gmail.com

11

A Legacy of Giving Back

Dr. Lamata Mitchell

AS A DESCENDENT of immigrants, I understand all too well the challenges that come with being identified as "other."

But that didn't stop my family from instilling within me the importance of a college education (I have two master's degrees and a doctorate) and its power to open doors that otherwise remain closed.

I am convinced the community college is a powerful tool for transforming lives. That belief informs my purpose to be a mentor to others and to make sure everyone has access to a college education regardless of their background—and that the educators and students I serve both now and in the future have the opportunity to experience the vast benefits of mentorship.

Like all immigration stories, mine is unique. My mother and her siblings came to England from Jamaica in the early 1960's, just a few years after my grandparents, William and Linda, had paved the way for our family to journey from the Caribbean to help England rebuild after World War II. My mother began working as a legal secretary, but she left that profession to go to nursing school to be a pediatric nurse and then had me a few years later.

I know little about my father because he passed away before I got to know him. Subsequently, I was raised by my mother and maternal grandparents, though, really, it was her brothers, my five uncles, who took it upon themselves to help take care of me since several years would pass before my mother remarried. One uncle in particular had a calming influence, always listened, and was not perturbed when I went through the up-and-down emotions of my teen years. His presence in my life meant a lot to me, especially during my preteens when I was trying to form my identity in a society where I did not see many who looked like me in leadership positions. You could say he was my first mentor.

When I first went to middle school in Nottingham, England, I quickly realized I was the only one in the all-girls school that looked like me in terms of color. For the first couple of years, that was a challenge. I was not invited to birthday parties or social events. Others just weren't used to having this black girl thrust into their social space. I was certainly not your typical Brit even though I was born in England. For instance, I grew up listening to Motown and was completely oblivious to British musicians like The Beatles or The Rolling Stones. Nor was I really expose to British cuisine because I had a godmother from India, so I grew up on that cuisine, as well as on the Jamaican dishes my grandparents cooked. Instead of Yorkshire pudding and a roast, our Sunday dinner was rice and peas, jerk chicken, and a glass of homemade spicy ginger beer. It was a remarkable contrast to the bland fare I encountered in the school cafeteria. Therefore, I was sort of ostracized both for my looks and because I was being raised by a family whose culture and traditions were far different than my peers. The British culture I was born into expected me to assimilate, while the culture I inherited from my family expected me to both remember and honor my roots. So, I was left to try to navigate these two worlds, making sure I was not defined by how other people saw me, or by their definitions of me, as I moved in and out of both worlds.

I continue to be intentional about that. I like the freedom of navigating from a margin that overlaps both cultures, and I think at times it is very difficult for people to put me in a particular spot. I take ownership of determining what my identity might be at any given time. It's little wonder, then, that I was also the anomaly of my family, gravitating toward the arts instead of health or science. I loved theater. I loved reading literature and good storytelling because I believe in the importance of being able to tell one's own story. When I prepared for college, I decided to major in English and philosophy. I had no interest at all in teaching, even though both my high school principal and undergrad advisor said I'd be a great educator. I wanted to get paid for reading all day long, so I eventually went into the publishing world on Fleet Street in London, reading and preparing manuscripts for publication.

In between finishing my first graduate degree and getting the job on Fleet Street, I was asked to help teach English at a private boarding school. Every student in the 16-year-old group I taught ended up passing the national test for English composition and literature. It was the first time that had ever happened at that school. But my first love remained publishing. At age 27, I was prompted to come to the United States to study American literature, with a concentration on

The Purpose and Power of Mentorship

African American literature, after working on one of Maya Angelou's manuscripts. As part of my studies, I was asked to teach again; this time, it was a composition class. I had a great time watching the students process what it meant to write well and to clearly articulate themselves on paper.

That planted a seed that came to full fruition years later when I taught Shakespeare at Rock Valley Community College in Rockford, Illinois. I taught for them as an adjunct for a couple of years before applying for and receiving a full-time instructor position. It was then that my passion for the value of community college education was born and nurtured.

From my upbringing, I have determined that I want to be judged on who I am as an individual and by my character, not by how others think I should fit in. Many of the community college students I encounter today from other countries are refugees or are first generation Americans. I am able to connect with these students, and other students who find themselves having to navigate two worlds or cultures, because of my own experiences. I understand the challenges of trying to navigate two worlds, and be accepted in both, without losing one's own identity in the process. I'll never forget when one of my very first community college students, a young woman with three children under five years of age, came to me one day to say she was going to have to drop out of school. Her husband had left her, and he was refusing to help with financial support. She was in tears, and when she explained her situation to me, I called a friend who is an attorney and asked if she would take her case.

I then told the student that I needed her to stay in school. "If you drop out," I told her, "your husband will win, and you'll continue the cycle of dependency and continued mistreatment by him, and your children will grow up thinking that is normal." We got her legal representation, she was able to stay in school, and a couple of years later she transferred to a four-year institution. Today, she is a registered nurse. She discovered that she had worth as a talented, strong woman who had much to contribute to society.

My background and my passion for helping others discover their purpose and capabilities, of course, informs my mentoring, particularly of women who are dealing with gender biases in their workplaces. In education, I'd anticipate seeing more females at the administration level, but it is still men who primarily fill these positions of leadership. For these women, it's another example of being identified as "other." As I mentor young ladies, I've seen them raise their hands in meetings and wait to be acknowledged while everyone keeps talking. The men leap into the conversation without raising their hands or waiting. So, I advise the women to wait for a pause and then speak up. "Don't put up your hands," I tell them. "They are not even looking at you because they are so engaged in what they are saying." Women are "talked over" all the time, so I tell them to jump in. "Don't get loud. Don't get shrill. Don't get angry. Just keep talking," I say. "Eventually, they will realize there is another voice and pause to hear what that voice is saying." I've discovered that women must learn to adapt to survive in anything they do, but they should do so in a very graceful and collaborative way.

As I mentor women, it also surprises me that they tend to be hesitant to proceed, and I find myself gently nudging them onward more than I do with male mentees. Men are ready and want me to tell them when to jump. Women tend to ask, "Do I have to? I'm not sure." I respond, "You *are* ready. Just take that step with confidence." I think this comes from the way many women are raised. Women are taught, "Don't be loud. Don't yell. Don't scream. Don't be vocal. Don't speak unless spoken to. Don't, don't, don't." I have found, especially in meetings, that if a woman is passionate about something, she is considered to be a pain, while if a man is passionate, he is thought of as being assertive. That said, I tell women that they do not have to act like a man to be accepted. I exhort them instead to act like themselves, and to be confident, firm, and true to who they are. As a mentor, I have to discern when to push and when to step back and let the ladies move forward a little bit on their own. When they respond, it is so empowering to them and exciting for me.

In the academic world, mentorship is vital because I work with a lot of gifted instructors who don't realize they have the ability to influence lives beyond the classroom through their leadership. They accept the fact that they can help a student learn, but when I identify an instructor as having leadership potential beyond what he or she does each day as an educator, the person is amazed. The person has already demonstrated the competencies and has a gift for leadership without recognizing it. I welcome the opportunity to mentor such individuals toward that potential.

Recently, I have been mentoring people who are thinking of moving into the next step of their career. My role is to help them see what they need to work on or think through how to take that step. I am also mentoring those who have inherited teams that need to work on becoming a cohesive, well-working group. Interestingly, when women inherit such teams, they sometimes struggle a bit more than men in a similar position with bringing that team together. I'm not always sure why that is, and I sometimes wonder if it's because women tend to be hesitant about their own leadership ability. They often second guess themselves or appear timid in their leadership.

A few years ago, I mentored two women, each of whom were educational leaders of gender-mixed teams, who encountered both men and women undermining or questioning their directives. I worked with them on how to push back by being more assertive without coming across as too aggressive (or the B-word). When they asked me how I seem to manage similar situations so calmly, I told them, "You might think that I navigate it with success and smoothness, but others would say, 'No, not so much. She can be a little confrontational.'" My mentoring with them focused more on the importance of being courageous instead of hesitant for fear of backlash. I really don't care about being confrontational because that isn't my intent. I try to be respectful and attentive to what people are saying as well as to the context and subtext of their comments, but it's a balance for me. In addition, I am not afraid of failure or of breaking the rules if it gets us to think outside of the box. So, when I am mentoring women, my goal is to help them find their voice and their own leadership style without feeling they need to mimic or duplicate somebody else's style. They need to be authentic in their own leadership.

The Purpose and Power of Mentorship

When someone asks me to mentor them, I always ask them to identify what they see in me that makes them identify me as a mentor. That helps me gauge, my approach, what they are looking for, and what they expect of me. Next, I share my expectations of them—what I refer to as the four "E's." I need them to bring *energy* to the process, since no one wants to be around someone who is whining and complaining that they don't want to do what is needed to progress. I want them to then be able to *energize* others through what they learn, *execute* the plan that we set out to achieve, and have the *edge* to make the tough decisions required to improve themselves and others.

We then schedule a set time to meet, which serves to help them prioritize the mentoring process, and I emphasize that I want to hear whatever it is they feel they want to share about an accomplishment or concern. "Tell me what is really in your heart of hearts," I say. "If there was nothing holding you back, who would you be as a person and what would you do?" I desire to push them out of the comfort zone of only sharing what they feel is safe or only sharing what makes them look appealing or acceptable. "As your mentor, I am not necessarily your friend," I tell them. "Your friend is going to accept you with all of your flaws and your weaknesses. A mentor is here to beat that out of you so you can be the very best *you* possible."

Finally, because I am investing time in them, I expect them to identify at least one other person that they are, in turn, willing to invest time in by being their mentor. We are all diamonds in the rough. It's that idea of, "Each one, teach one." I will not mentor someone who only thinks about themselves and what they can get out of a partnership. Not only is that very self-centered, but I don't think that helps society move forward or bond as a community. If someone is only going into a relationship for what they can get out of it, they have all the wrong incentives and motives to begin with.

One of my first students at Rock Valley Community College understood this expectation. When he first took my class, I noticed that he struggled and stumbled over the words every time I asked for volunteers to read something out loud. One day, I pulled him aside and asked, "Have you been diagnosed with a reading disability?" He responded, "No, not that I know of. Reading is hard for me, and English is hard for me." I suggested he should have his mother set up an appointment for him to be tested. Sure enough, he was diagnosed with dyslexia. When he came back to class, he said, "You were right. I have this problem, so you should give me less work to do."

"Absolutely not," I replied, and then revealed something to him. "I struggle with the same thing, so I am going to share the coping mechanisms my mother taught me so you can be successful." I mentored him throughout his time at the school, and I always told him I was going to invest in him, but I needed a return. I needed him to invest in others.

He is now married with four beautiful children, and two years ago, I had the honor of being on his dissertation committee. He now has a doctorate in education, he is employed as a middle school principal, and he is a mentor to his students.

In recent years, I have started mentoring a younger age group: 11- to 15-year-olds. I'm not sure these young people even know what a "mentor" is, but their parents do, and they recognize its value. They'll ask me to talk to their son or daughter, and before I know it, I will have formed a relationship with that person. I love to check in on them, too. "How are you doing?" "What are you thinking?" "How is school going?" "Have you thought of that?" "Did you read this?" I just love bright young people who are excited about life and the opportunities it has for them, and who want to do something positive with those opportunities. I love the way their smiles light up their faces, and I find that once they get to know me, they begin to take off that hard exterior and become themselves.

I tend to talk more about "edge" with these teens and preteens because they feel so pressured by their peers. I'll ask them, "Do you have the edge to make a decision by yourself, and to do what you know is the right thing to do, even though the rest of the group doesn't?" I tell them it's okay not to follow the crowd, but to just "be you and find out who you are." We also talk about self-worth. They are bombarded by the media telling them how they should think, how they should look, and what is and isn't acceptable. This is a challenge for young ladies of color, in particular, because they don't often see themselves reflected in a positive light. Rather than taking on the burden of trying to remake themselves so they fit in, I encourage them to be true to themselves because they are fearfully and wonderfully made (Psalm 139:14), and there is a reason they are on this earth. God is not finished with them yet.

I've had three significant mentors in my life. One is the president of a college in Michigan. She's quite the opposite of me: quiet, very thoughtful, and I can't always read what is going through her mind by her facial expressions. She is

A Legacy of Giving Back

calm while I'm all in the thick of it, rolling my sleeves up and asking whether or not we need to arm wrestle over something. She has taught me about having grace under fire. She is often in public situations where something can be easily misunderstood or misconstrued, yet when others go in for the attack against her, she never retaliates. She just lets them have their say and thanks them for their observation. It has been a blessing for me to see that other perspective on how to respond when someone challenges me on a matter.

The second mentor's number one strength is wooing others. When he and I go out somewhere together, I know that I am going to meet everybody in that room, whether I want to or not. I am going to know their names, and they are going to know all about me. I am more of an introvert, so by the end of the gathering I am worn out, but I have learned from him that personal warmth and genuine love of people is such an important part of leadership. Because of his mentorship, I now make an effort to meet everybody when I go into a room. I get to connect with people and usually encounter someone I would not have had the opportunity to meet otherwise.

The final mentor is also very quiet and thoughtful. She thinks carefully before she speaks, and she will research something thoroughly before making a final decision. What I have learned from her, in particular, is the importance of having people quite the opposite of yourself around you so that you can grow and move forward. She once told me, "If you are always looking for people that are just like you, you are going to lose wonderful opportunities of creativity and innovation." She's absolutely right.

My mentoring style is largely intuitive. I follow my

The Purpose and Power of Mentorship

instincts, but when I think about mentoring I often tell myself, "I wish someone had told me about this (i.e. the value of being mentored) when I was 20 or taken me under their wings then." I truly believe it is my duty to help and give back in any way that I can. It would be wrong of me to have the advantage of being helped by someone and not share that with others. I honestly don't think I would be able to sleep at night or look at myself in the mirror if I didn't give back to society by helping others.

It partly comes from having a grandfather who constantly asked me, "What are you giving back to society?" Back when I was a teenager, the answer to that question was absolutely nothing. "What do you mean, 'What am I giving back?'" I'd sass. "You should ask the world what else it is going to give me." Thankfully, as I matured, I began to understand what he was asking, and now it's a legacy he has passed on to me. His advice, "If your hands are always closed, God can't put anything else in them," now resonates with me.

I wish more people would selflessly give of their knowledge, and of their lives, with others and take a risk on those they are willing to mentor. What keeps us from doing this, I think, is fear of failure or of making a mistake. But that's because we don't tend to see failure as an opportunity to learn something new. I also don't believe we really take the time to get to know people. We can be very superficial. We are so busy with our own lives and accomplishments that we don't take the time to ask, "Who else can I bring forward with me? Who else can I help?"

As we go through life, we should always ask ourselves, "What is my legacy? What would I like to be remembered for?" On a tombstone, where the dash comes between the

A Legacy of Giving Back

year you were born and the year that you are put to rest, what do you want that dash to represent?

If you touch just one life, it will have a ripple effect that will blow your mind with its legacy of giving back to all the "others" you encounter along the way.

Dr. Lamata Mitchell serves as the Assistant Vice Chancellor for Student Learning at Pima Community College in Tucson, AZ. With shared oversight for instruction and academic operational services across a multi-campus district, she provides leadership and support for administrators, faculty, and staff in order to ensure the college's mission and vision for student success are being met. Lamata holds a doctorate of philosophy in English from Northern Illinois University, a master's degree in English from Andrews University, and a master's degree in publishing and journalism from Loughborough University. Contact Lamata at lamatamitchell31@gmail.com

12

Blessed to be a Blessing

Dr. Karockas Watkins

BORN TO A 15-year-old mother, we lived in the projects and got by on generic brand cheese, peanut butter, and powdered milk purchased with government-issued food stamps. Yet my mom, Johnnie, always told me I could become anything I wanted to be. She said, "Do not let what you see dictate what you could be."

I never forgot that. I worked hard with a single-minded motivation to not be in the projects. To not be poor. To not be a person with no influence. I went to school, discovered I was good in math and science, and got good grades.

Today, I like to think my parents are pretty proud of me. After all, I am a blessed man.

I serve as chief executive officer, president, and executive director of Ability Plus Inc. in Huntsville, AL, the largest single provider in Alabama of services for people with special needs. When I took over as CEO four years ago, we changed the culture. In a year-and-a-half, we dramatically turned around that culture, and the company's bottom line, through teaching and mentorship. I also serve as CEO/president of Vision Excellence Company. We specialize in leadership and business development consulting and seminars. I've had the joy and privilege to work with major automakers, defense contractors, and churches, and I have spoken in 32 different countries around the world. As board overseer of Emmanuel: The Connection Church in Madison, AL, I preach almost every Sunday and oversee the ministry. Since I became an ordained minister over 30 years ago, I have traveled around the world and done mission work (I like to call it, "empowerment" work), including going to the continent of Africa 25 times. At one point I was overseeing about 400 African pastors.

Like I said, I am a blessed man—especially through my wife, Audra, who grew up three houses down from me, and our three wonderful kids: Brianna, who was a Bill Gates Millennium Scholar and is now getting ready to go to law school; Christian, who is in college studying to be a teacher; and my teenage son, Joshua, who is seeing and learning the value of hard work from his parents and his two older sisters. My wife and I tell all three, "You've got to be all you can be—and you need people helping you along the way."

That's the power of mentorship: people helping you get to your destiny.

Another facet of my blessing in life are the two mentors who have helped me along the way. First was Dr. David Green, Jr., dean of the science and math department at Kettering University (formerly GMI Engineering & Management Institute) in Michigan before he retired. He chose me from a slate of students in Alabama to go to the General Motors Institute to further my original career as an engineer. He mentored me all five of the years I was there, and even when I wanted to quit, he challenged me to stay. He said he knew greatness was inside of me—something that I kind of felt back then but wasn't convinced was totally real. I didn't think that I could live up to it. Dr. Green didn't give me an out. He forced me to buckle down and do what I had to do. His tenacious guidance propelled me to an engineering career that saw me work at General Motors and IBM before returning to General Motors to close out that phase of my professional life and transition into what I'm doing today.

Second was Dr. Maurice K. Wright. He has been my pastor for over 25 years and is my spiritual father. He sits on the board at Ability Plus, and he has been a sounding board every time I've needed one. He is one of the wisest men I have ever known, and he constantly encouraged me, saying that I was special, and that God had a special calling on my life that I couldn't run from. "You can't deny it," he said. "You have to embrace it." He always told me to welcome the opportunities that came my way and to never feel like I didn't deserve them, because I did.

That is the power of mentors: individuals who support you and speak into you so that you can be positioned to succeed by fulfilling your destiny.

There are three distinct ways I take what I have been blessed with to be a blessing to others. I am a business mentor, a leadership mentor to several domestic and international leaders, and an executive/leadership/life coach serving individual leaders, corporations, and non-profits. My role as a coach is to talk to others about their goals, their dreams, and their visions for themselves and for their company. I then help them come up with strategies for what they want to do and discuss the difficulties in making those things come to pass. My role as a coach is not to tell them what to do. It is to talk them through what is already inside of them. They already have the answers. I help bring those to the forefront and make them tangible. We may be smart, but all of us have blind spots. My job is to reveal those blind spots so they can deal with anything that affects them in a negative way.

As a coach, I once worked with an organization that had the talent, but the culture was bad. No one believed in what they thought they could do. As a result, the company was failing and was about to be shut down. I started with the head person in that organization and asked him, "How do you see leadership?" He told me he had never really thought about it, though he believed he had a very dictatorship-type style. We talked about the positives and the negatives of that style and came to the conclusion that it was not best for the business he was running. We talked about him becoming a servant leader and doing things he would never have done otherwise, such as approaching workers, asking them how they are doing, and focusing on how the team could go forward instead of dictating how he was going to make the company better. He had to fight off a great deal of self-arrogance and pride, and we coached through it.

After about six months, his people started seeing him in a different light. When they found out his heart, mind, and resources were invested in them and supporting them, things started to change. In the process, I saw both him and his top leaders alter how they had always done things. Together, they addressed many negative issues that he had previously known nothing about. We talked not about problems, but opportunities, and then I watched them teach their departments how to address those opportunities and model it before them. It was fascinating and fulfilling to see the results!

Business mentorship is differentiated from leadership mentorship because it is a strategy. Leadership is involved, of course, but business mentorship calls for looking at that company's model, profit margins, and desired outcomes and determining what needs to be done next. Two vital questions to consider are, "What kind of talent do you have in your business to do what you say you want to do?" and "Are the right people on the bus in the right seats?" One of my giftings is placing the right people on the bus in the right seat.

I worked with a company that's number one in the nation in insurance marketing. I met with their executives, and we went through their business structure all the way down to every salaried person in the corporation. We changed who reported to who and why, and we gave people different roles according to their strengths. My task is to look at the totality of the business: who is there, what do they do, where do they go, and what are the strategies and goals that need to be put into place in order to achieve what they want to do? When I came on at Ability Plus, I incorporated business mentorship techniques, and it changed who we were and how we responded to our customers. More often than not, businesses need to change the model because the model has a culture which determines how people act and respond. You can't work on the people until you have worked on the culture, and you can't work on the culture until you have worked on the model.

I have had the privilege during my career to receive business mentorship. While dealing with an issue that affected my future with a company, my business mentor led me in a very positive direction. His mentorship allowed me to look deep within myself to access my "why" in life and business. Several business opportunities were in front of me, and I was struggling with reasons to move ahead with one of them. Because of his business experience and his wisdom, I was given good information so I could make a positive decision.

Finally, leadership mentorship is one-on-one. It's all about the person, how their personality fits in with who they are leading, and how they can make those around them better by bettering themselves. It is not about the business, although it will affect the business. It is about the person. I focus on self-inspection. I check up from the neck up and look around from the shoulder down. I exhort their strengths and have them work on their problems. This requires honesty. I ask, "Have you developed a habit of learning and reading?" "How are you building yourself?" One of my most successful leadership mentorship clients is Dr. Timothy Ifedioranma of Nigeria. I've visited him 18 times over the last 20 years. He is a lawyer. He is a pastor. He is a bishop—and currently he is a congressperson for his country. In working with him, encouraging him, and talking about strategy with him, Dr. Ifedioranma has done quite well. At last count, 120 different churches are under his authority. I have given him hope and encouragement to stay the course and stay true to his core values: who he is and his "why" for living. For any of us, if we do something that goes outside of our "why," we shouldn't be doing it.

One of my greatest honors was to lead a young man in his journey to fulfill his life dream of owning his own business. This gentleman was struggling with who he was after being reminded of the many negatives of his past. Together, we went through his strengths and weaknesses so that he could see he had incredible gifts and the ability to be successful in his dream. I used several emotional intelligence (EI) techniques to bring him greater self-awareness and self-management. He not only listened, but he applied the knowledge gained in our leadership sessions. He is currently doing a great job fulfilling his passion.

At the end of the day, I believe every mentor needs a mentee, and every mentee needs a mentor. Every person needs that someone—who has done more than them or who they are trying to be like—who can speak into their lives and model things that are going to work. Mentorship can be done one-on-one, with a group, or in a seminar, but we need people to mentor us because we are designed to sharpen our skills. Mentorship refines who we are to be the best we can be.

I'll never forget when a mentor of mine helped me through a time of uncertainty. I was at a crossroads in my career and needed direction on what to do next. I had established a solid reputation in various influential circles and had done well leading the company where I was employed. Yet I felt like it was time to move forward and do something different. I just didn't know how. My mentor asked me some pinpoint questions concerning my passion and where I saw myself in the future. I hadn't been asked about either one in quite a long time. Because of his genuine interest and caring, those questions caused me to look deeper within me than I had in years. I knew he was asking what I *wanted* to do, not what I could do or what would make me the most money. He was asking me to unveil what I truly wanted to pursue in the last phase of my work life. His guidance helped me to find my heartbeat once again. He was like a boxing trainer assisting a fighter who had been swinging, dancing, and taking and dishing out blows, but was getting fuzzy and needed to refocus. I gained new clarity to know exactly how to battle and finish the fight. I truly believe what we did together will reshape the coming decade. My next 10 years won't look like the last 10. I can't remember being this excited about the opportunities and the possibilities.

Pursuing your passion is so important. I ask other people about passion all the time, and I even teach a series called "Chase Passion and Purpose." So, what do you want to do with your life? I believe every person has an element of greatness within them that can only be brought out with proper mentorship, coaching, and encouragement. All of us possess blind spots that only others can see and bring out of us. It's like the person in the gym that does eight reps on a machine, and the trainer says, "You can get two more." You will never get those two more on your own without a mentor or coach who is pushing you. If you are willing to be great and you really want to reach your maximum potential, you must have mentorship or coaching. It's not an "if." It's not a choice. It's a must if you are going to be successful.

My favorite book of all time says one can chase a thousand, but two can put ten thousand to flight (Deuteronomy 32:30). We are better together. We will do more together. Mentorship brings people together so that one who is blessed can be a blessing to the other—and what is more powerful than that?

Blessed to be a Blessing

Dr. Karockas Watkins serves as a leadership mentor to several domestic and international leaders, and he is the chief executive officer, president, and executive director of Ability Plus Inc. in Huntsville, AL. He is also CEO/president of Vision Excellence Company, a leadership and business consulting company, board overseer of Emmanuel: The Connection Church in Madison, AL, and a business mentor, and executive/leadership/life coach. Contact Karockas at karockas.watkins@ability-plus.org or karockas@vision-excellence-company.com

13

Full Circle

Odetta Scott

ONE OF MY driving forces as a woman and as a leader, in order to fulfill my God-given passion to better myself and others, is the saying "each one reach one"—and there's truly no better way to live out that saying than through mentorship.

Mentoring is about striking a relationship with another person, listening to their needs, and meeting them where they are so that I can share my experience or insightful reflections, be a sounding board to them, and help them better themselves and those they influence.

It's my personal passion come full circle.

My experiences of leaving my home in Vicksburg, Mississippi in eleventh grade to attend a magnet school in Columbus, Mississippi to enhance my education developed and grew my spiritual life, deepened my faith, and allowed me to learn the value of relationships with others. I found myself seeking those who had gone through similar experiences who could help me navigate the new and different situations I encountered. I was among a group of students away from home and still growing into adults, and I was able to develop a relationship with someone who had also left home early and made it through successfully. I had tons of questions. "How did you do it?" "What was the biggest challenge?" "How did you deal with loneliness?" In addition, I formed relationships with peers and classmates, and we managed to excel in school, become stronger, and help the next class of students adjust and succeed.

From there, I attended the U.S. Naval Academy in Annapolis, Maryland through my sophomore year before moving on to Texas A&M University to finish college and earn my degree in mechanical engineering technology in 1995. One of my distant cousins, Ms. Brown, was a vital mentor to me, though neither of us recognized it at the time. She always ensured that I cultivated dreams, thoughts, and plans to have a positive impact on myself and others. In our times together, we discussed her path and the things that she had learned, good and bad, along the way. That helped me to pause and reevaluate my actions. When my original desire to become an astronaut, inspired by Mae Jemison (the first female African American to go into space) did not go as planned, Ms. Brown was the one who encouraged me to have a solid back-up plan. If I hadn't had those conversations and reflections with her, I may not have transferred from the U.S. Naval Academy to Texas A&M, and I don't know if I would've gone on to achieve what I have today. I am so grateful to her.

As a mentor, I have been positioned to aid in the development of individuals through my activities with organizations such as Advancing Minorities Interest in Engineering, the Society of Women Engineers, and as a Science, Technology, Engineering, and Mathematics (STEM) ambassador. I've also done this through my 20-plus years of work experience in aerospace and defense, from mechanical design through program management, and in my current position as a senior leader at a Fortune 500 aerospace company, where I'm responsible for developing and implementing strategy for non-product supplier performance excellence.

I believe to be a successful mentor, you have to be self-aware of many things: your performance, your triggers, and what I call "your goods and your not-so-goods" so that you can take that understanding of yourself and use it to help your mentees build and develop themselves well. This gives them the opportunity to learn from your mistakes and not repeat them in their own lives. I recently mentored Angela through a situation where I thought she was being treated unfairly. In working with Angela, I drew from a past experience with a previous employer where I was brought in to help a director whose programs were hemorrhaging, and we needed to stop the bleeding. After my initial assessment, I determined that the best I could do was slow down the damage through containment and risk mitigation activities. Yet the director and I were like oil and water. Our styles did not mesh.

One day, it got to the point where I had to have a courageous conversation with him to get set on roles and responsibilities as well as establish a proper mode of operation. During our conversation, he agreed that we indeed had two different styles and that the team needed more of my collaborative, seek-to-understand style instead of his dictatorial approach.

The Purpose and Power of Mentorship

Everyone moved forward to do the best they could to meet the deliverable and still be a positive, high performing team.

When I shared this story with Angela, she related to it, as things were not going well with her programs. She decided she needed to have a conversation with her management to drive awareness and see if they could align on roles, responsibilities, and the best path forward. A couple of weeks later, Angela gave me an update and felt it had positive results. Her manager respected her more, and the team appreciated her stepping in.

When I mentor, I've learned to be patient, to be present, and to actively listen. When someone is talking to me, they will usually say something that causes my mind to start formulating a response or solution when, instead, I should put that on pause and hear them out first. That allows me to be more empathetic to where they are and where they may be going so that I can best help them. I am in an ongoing mentoring relationship with a colleague, Joseph. He is a sharp engineer and is considered to have high potential within the organization because he has managed to grow his career quickly as compared to others. We once traveled together internationally, and we needed to share some large electronic files with our international counterparts, Jade and Gene. We discussed the best way to share the content, and I recommended a technique that had been successful for me previously. However, Joseph didn't think it would work, so we did not try it at that time. I pulled him aside seeking to understand his concerns, learn his idea, and get his thoughts on how long he thought it would it take to get the information out.

As we talked, he confessed he had rejected my idea because he didn't know how to use it. If I hadn't listened or sought to understand and address his concerns, we would've gone in a different direction. By actively listening to Joseph, we were able to gain alignment and proceed. It made us both stronger. Joseph further shared with me that he does not have empathy. He is one of the smartest individuals I know, yet he struggles with connecting with others and meeting people where they are. As a father to very young children and an engineer in a growing corporation, Joseph understands that can have a negative impact both personally and professionally. I encouraged Joseph that he needed to learn how to actively listen and seek to understand others to make a connection with them.

The most common themes or subjects that come up as I mentor others are self-awareness, continuous improvement, and encouragement to spur their success. Another one of the people I mentor is Jean, a female executive in the male-dominated aerospace and defense industry. She was dealing with a common struggle for a female leader: a tendency to feel like she had to be perfect and even overcompensate to be respected and heard. In her case and similar ones I have encountered, I counsel reframing (the ability to take a scenario or a situation and express it differently) by saying, "You are enough, but what I need you to do is get out of your own way so you can be better positioned to think about the things that make you different and add value, and then speak from those things." Understanding and declaring what differentiates you is a leadership characteristic that works regardless of gender. "You just have to go in and be you," I say. "If you continue to be you, they will see that value."

It took me about three months or so of repeatedly beating that drum to set up that cadence in her life, but now Jean feels it, believes it, and acts on it. She is a great leader and is very humble. Though it has taken some time, Jean is now doing well in reframing her situation. Instead of focusing on what she doesn't bring and what she can't do, she is focusing on what she can bring and do. I often ask Jean to see what sets her apart from others. Her unique style of authentic leadership, her ability to meet others where they are and support and encourage them in their own abilities is unparalleled. I see it, others she has mentored see it, and other executives in the organization see it. That awareness has made a tremendous difference.

I believe there are distinctions to be drawn between mentoring, coaching, and sponsorship. Mentoring is a partnership between two people (mentor and mentee) normally working in a similar field or sharing similar experiences. The mentor focuses on building capability and meeting a person where they are by providing support, encouragement, guidance, and ideas to help the mentee reach professional goals. They may share their personal knowledge and experiences with the mentee to help promote self-discovery.

Coaching is more task oriented and includes taking feedback about a specific performance activity. A coach can be provided in a more formal structured relationship using a set agenda to reinforce or change skills and behaviors. Oftentimes, the words mentoring and coaching are used interchangeably, and there can be some overlap, but they are really not the same thing.

Sponsorship is all about who is wearing my t-shirt when I am not in the room. Who is advocating for me to ensure that I am at least considered for a position that, perhaps, I don't even know about? A mentor or coach doesn't necessarily become a sponsor, but they can when a win-win situation presents itself where the person is in a position of influence and is able to advocate for you and your skill set and performance.

I coached a young lady, Tammy, who aspired to take on a different role within her company. She had about 80 percent of the skills needed for that role, so our challenge was to obtain the remaining skill set she needed from the competencies toolkit she already possessed. Again, I used reframing. In this scenario it was not as much about the title given to the roles she had previously held, but the results and actions she had taken in carrying out those roles. Just because she didn't have the formal title for the roles didn't mean she couldn't do them. Together, Tammy and I reframed her thought processes and approach. We held a couple of mock interviews to ensure she was confident about what she brought to the table, and she got the job! It is always a great feeling to help others reach their goals and dreams.

Mentoring, coaching, and sponsorship are essential in a corporate setting, as is your own personal "board of directors." This board is comprised of those who are in your inner circle, a very small group, or nucleus, of individuals who will tell you like it is and are truly authentic to help you navigate through your blind spots and provide insight. People may not sit on your board of directors indefinitely. You may need them for a shorter period of time. When discerning who should sit on your board of directors, look for that natural draw, or notion, that tells you if you are going to connect with them or not. It usually takes a while for that relationship to form, but over time you can identify those folks who are going to be willing and open to serve in that capacity. In the end, their priority should be to help you be the best you can be.

The Purpose and Power of Mentorship

Jennifer sits on my board of directors, and I consider her a godsend. She helps me to see my blind spots and is not shy about sharing her feedback with me. One nugget she gave me was the realization that whenever it seemed everyone had initially bought in to my vision, that didn't ensure true alignment and, therefore, I often shut down. The fact that I did not ask probing questions to address their concerns made the implementation of my vision take longer than needed. It was eye opening, and I am getting better at this. I also carried her insight over to my mentoring and coaching. When I hear myself asking those same kinds of probing questions to others, I can't help but smile. Jennifer helped me shore up a blind spot. She's priceless.

When I have been mentored by others, I've learned the benefit of being open as a mentee and accepting my mentors' feedback as a gift. No one is perfect. It is all about the learning—and even though I have been mentoring others for years, there is still much for me to learn from my own mentors. For example, I may have biases that I can identify and address in a safe place with my mentors to help me grow and mature. The two most impactful mentors in my life have been Rebecca Stoner, the person who hired me for the company where I'm currently employed, and Dr. Amanda H. Goodson, who, of course, is featured in this book. With Amanda, the consistency of our engagement, and the tons of expertise she has shared with me openly and willingly, has helped me think through challenges and build my own mentoring muscle so I can go and do the same to strengthen others. Rebecca allowed me to leverage her 20-plus years of experience to get up to speed and quickly accelerate after coming from a very different corporation in the same industry. She, too, was a consistent voice in my life, and though I no longer report to her, we still have helpful conversations in what is now a mutually beneficial relationship professionally and personally.

Thanks to Amanda, Rebecca, and others who have poured of themselves into me over the years, I know that it still goes back to "each one reach one" as we look for opportunities to position ourselves and others to navigate to their destiny. There's plenty of expertise to go around. We just have to help each other. This requires vulnerability and a willingness to be transparent and let others in. That's not always easy, but it is worth it.

You did not get to where you are alone. Take a moment and reflect on that, then use that feeling to pay it forward and help at least one other person through mentoring, coaching, or sponsorship. Start with just one, and I guarantee you'll develop a desire to help others.

Odetta Scott is an author, advisor, mentor, and lecturer who has fueled the development of individuals at all levels as well as driven transformational culture in professional and business settings. Contact Odetta at http://linkedin.com/in/odetta-scott-58298513

14

Profound Effect

P. Leon King

WHETHER IT WAS when I was drafted into the United States Army, served as a community volunteer, worked with clients as a financial consultant, or any other number of times before and since, mentorship has played a pivotal role in my life. It has been essential. It has been educational. It has been humbling and rewarding.

Most of all, it has helped me make a difference in the lives of others.

After all, people see us every day—and our example has a profound effect on them.

As founder and managing partner of K-WAM Financial Solutions, I work with veterans and leaders with minority-owned companies who are doing business with federal and state government agencies. I do a great deal of mentoring in the lending process. It is my responsibility to make sure business owners get the money they are looking to acquire for the best deals possible. In order to do that, I have to bring my clients up to speed on borrowing and lending,

The Purpose and Power of Mentorship

and help them understand the responsibilities and accountability they have in the loan's terms and conditions. A lot of small business owners specialize in a particular area of skill or giftedness, but they're generally not experts in finance. I strive to bridge that gap, and that requires mentoring and guiding the client through most phases of the process.

In my line of work, it's not unusual for me to seek some mentoring of my own along the way so that I can best serve the needs of my clients. I was working with one business owner on an offer received from an alternate investing group. I was dismayed because it was a rather large deal, and I was in a quandary about how I should approach it. I wrestled with it all morning before calling a lifelong friend who was a real estate agent. I posed the dilemma to him, and we had a great conversation. I came away with a sense of direction and felt strongly that his consultation was worthwhile.

That's what mentoring does, even if it's just over a single phone call. It makes you better, and it enables you to help others improve themselves and realize their goals.

My very first specific mentorship experience came when I was 11 years old. I procured a job at Charlie's Grocery Store a half block from my house. I wanted to contribute to our household finances as well as make some money for myself. Charlie had a way about him, a kindness and compassion, that he showed to me and to our customers. While he taught me to stock shelves and perform customer service duties, he also showed me what to look for and expect from people. I learned from him that just because someone looks

Profound Effect

different from me does not mean they are cruel or hostile. He went above and beyond to help me and his customers in ways no one else would. That stuck with me. As I grew older, I came to recognize how valuable my time with Charlie was. He didn't just show me how to do a job, but he taught me what kinds of people to learn from and grow under.

In my early years, I began working on a horse farm and riding academy. Weekends were our busiest time, and all of us worked long hours on Saturdays and Sundays. During the late fall and winter months, my friend Phil and I earned lunch money working as caddies at the local golf course on the weekend. The work ethic I gained through those experiences has also informed my mentoring and my professional abilities today. As a result of my time on the horse farm and caddying on weekends, I missed out on a lot of family and church activities between ages 12 and 16. The only reason I left the horse farm was to play on my high school football team. The owner of the farm refused to allow time off during the week for me to attend daily practices. Phil and I continued to caddie on Sundays, and during my junior and senior years in high school, I worked at Brandywine Raceway as a dishwasher, and the following year, as a construction laborer.

My personal faith and mentoring abilities were shaped in large part through the mentoring I have received from my wife, Sharon Wamble-King. Her faith and biblical knowledge were nurtured from childhood and broadened through her attendance and graduation from Bible college. I had much to learn from her, as my spiritual development differed dramatically from hers. Although I prayed often and told myself that I believed in God, I lacked the foundation on which faith stands. I attended and participated in church activities, and I felt that I possessed Christian attributes, but it wasn't until I met Sharon that I had someone with whom I could be honest and open with about the myriad of questions I didn't have answers to about God, the Bible, and some Christian traditions. Her mentorship is the underpinning of my Christian development, including my dedication to studying the Bible, sharing God's Word with others, leading Bible study discussion groups, and our own prayer partnership as husband and wife as we adopted God as the head of our home and the center of our lives. Throughout my life, I can see how God purposefully put people in my path (like Sharon) when He knew I needed them and was ready to learn and understand His love and will for me.

After I joined the U.S. Army in 1966, I was put to work in culinary school, first in California and then as a resident assistant in Virginia. Eventually, the head instructor asked me if I wanted to learn how to teach the program. My original role was as a supply clerk ordering all the food, tools, and equipment that the trainees needed to complete the eight-week training course. The instructor took me under his wing, I followed him, and I listened to the instructions he gave and how he went about teaching the trainees to read recipes and measure and mix ingredients. After about two weeks, he let me do it all for the first time. I presented him with a game plan every morning as to what was on the menu and the approach I'd take with the students to teach them to follow the recipes, understand serving times, and learn how the

Profound Effect

food was supposed to be displayed. He monitored me for the next couple of weeks before leaving me totally on my own.

Working my way through college, I spent time as an insurance agent back when an agent went home to home to collect monthly premiums. While my primary goal of these visits was to collect payments, I learned an unexpected skill: active listening. My clients told me their stories, and I learned a lot about them. As I listened to their difficulties and struggles, I gave my best effort in offering solutions and advice. I developed a sense not only of responsibility, but accountability. I wanted to share my insights and offer honest opinions.

I learned a new mentor-mentee dynamic back then. I also learned something during a finance class when I was invited into a conversation between the professor and one of the students. We traditionally think of a teacher being a mentor and a student being a mentee; in this instance, however, the student was offering information and advice about the stock market that the professor was unfamiliar with, which was eye-opening.

All of my previous learning experiences about life and mentorship served me well later on when I was working in health care administration at the University of California, San Francisco. In the early 1990's, the minister from my home church, Third Baptist Church, and a Jewish rabbi were collaborating to bring together the different ethnic communities in San Francisco. They sought me out to get my thoughts. Having discovered that mentorship can come from numerous places, some less-than-traditional, I was enthusiastic to share. I mentioned I was interested in launching an after-school tutorial program for elementary and high school students, and they created a task force and appointed me chair of the initiative. We called it "Back on Track," and it was hosted at

The Purpose and Power of Mentorship

Third Baptist and co-sponsored by the area Jewish Temple. In the first year alone, we brought 150 mentors from churches, downtown businesses, and the community together under one roof and matched them with 150 elementary and high school student mentees. Students and mentors alike came from all walks of life, and many of the students had never before had the opportunity to be mentored on a one-to-one basis. Students' grades and confidence levels improved, and the tutors gleaned a sense of satisfaction.

The Back On Track program ran from the mid-1980's to the mid-1990's, but some of those mentor-mentee relationships are still intact today. It was a beautiful thing to see the two congregations come together to sponsor a project that was beneficial to the community as a whole.

Simply put, mentoring is establishing a one-to-one relationship where two people come together to achieve a specific outcome. The mentor's role, first and foremost, is to listen to and understand who the mentee is, unveil and internalize their needs, issues, concerns, desires, and plans, and then develop a plan to execute each aspect and measure their success. In my business, I spend time mentoring people, even if they don't realize it. Someone might come to me with an idea of what they need—say, a budget of $10,000 to start a project—but no plan to execute their ideas or any long-term needs or goals. I help them make a plan that includes taking into account how much money they actually need if they consider other factors. I teach them how to plan for the next 12-month cycle, how and where to bank their assets, and how to stock and manage inventory. I also cover anticipating unforeseen consequences, generating enough revenue to pay back any loans while replenishing inventory, and any similar items they hadn't considered.

The most critical point of mentoring is to be a terrific observer because people can't always adequately express their concerns verbally. Their body language is helpful in providing a sense of how and when to speak and listen as a mentor. I've also learned to never go into a mentoring relationship with preconceived notions. As a mentor, you may know what you want to achieve, but how you'll get there can vary and will be unique for each mentee. If you go in thinking you are the be-all, know-all, you are not going to be successful. I believe I am who I am because that's the way God wanted it. I've been blessed with the ability to listen actively and to internalize and think about what people say and apply it. Especially as a mentor, I benefit from listening to what my mentees need. I even ask, "Is this helpful?" or "Is this useful?" Those questions and others help me to guide them in a way that works best for them.

When I first consider the legacy I'd like to leave behind on this earth, I know I want to develop K-WAM, or some other business enterprise, to be successful and capable of growth and continuation for many years, and then leave that for my children, grandchildren, and their children. Therefore, as a mentor, my desired legacy is similarly generational. As I stated earlier, others are watching us, and our example has a profound effect on them. They watch our lifestyle and how we conduct ourselves. They see what we do and what we write, particularly as it relates to what we post on social media. Therefore, we need to be cognizant of who we are, what kind of images we are projecting about ourselves, and how we are portraying ourselves.

I encourage you to set a goal to put God first, live a God-filled life, not be selfish in any way, and identify how and where you can help others. Be generous and considerate, and then look within yourself to see what you can give away that will impact and effectively influence those around you.

P. Leon King is founder and managing partner of K-WAM Financial Solutions. He launched K-WAM in 2005 with the goal of supporting the financial needs of veteran and minority-owned companies doing business with federal and state government agencies. Prior to launching K-WAM, Leon served as a financial consultant with Washington Mutual, and he also had a long career in health care administration at the University of California, San Francisco. Contact Leon at pleonking@comcast.net

15

The Best Version

Jeannie Lynch

I'M AN OLD Washington Redskins fan, and I love Vince Lombardi. What a lot of people do not know about the Hall of Fame National Football League coach, most famous for leading the Green Bay Packers to wins in the first two Super Bowl games, is that he coached the Redskins after his time with the Packers. My family had season tickets to all the Redskins games for years, and being an athlete myself, Lombardi will always have a special place in my heart because he was such an outstanding coach and person.

He once said, "There are a lot of coaches with good ball clubs who know the fundamentals and have plenty of discipline but still don't win the game. Then you come to the third ingredient: if you're going to play together as a team, you've got to care for one another. You've got to love each other. Each player has to be thinking about the next guy."

Lombardi concluded, "The difference between mediocrity and greatness is the feeling these guys have for each other."[1]

The same is true of mentorship: the difference between

mediocrity and greatness is the third ingredient. Caring for one another. Loving each other.

My goal as a mentor is to assist people in being the best version of themselves—and the only way I can do that is to meet them exactly where they are: in love, genuinely caring for them with no judgment. Mentorship is first about relationship and investing in that relationship.

Both of my parents were coaches and natural athletes themselves, and I definitely had my gifts in that area. I excelled in several sports, including golf, track, tennis, basketball, and softball. I even played competitive softball into my early thirties. Back when I was a young college student struggling to find my way in life as an athlete and as a person, I had the opportunity to have a great mentor. He was my volleyball coach, Terry Pettit. I was on scholarship to play basketball at Louisburg College in Louisburg, North Carolina, but Coach Pettit wanted me to play volleyball for him there as well. Thirteen of his 15 players had volleyball scholarships, but I walked on and had never touched a volleyball before. Within six weeks, I had earned a position on his starting squad. He saw the potential I had as a natural athlete and brought it out of me on the volleyball court. Coach Pettit often looked at me when I was practicing and said, just under his breath, "Do you have it?" I knew exactly what he was talking about and pursued "it," that extra edge, with everything I had.

I knew Coach Pettit genuinely cared about me. I would have run through a brick wall for that man. He encouraged me. He was honest, and he pushed me. He understood how to do all of those things and to what degree to do them. I was very respectful of him. When he told me to do something, I knew he knew his business, and I wanted to perform at my highest level. No wonder Terry Pettit went on lead the Nebraska Cornhuskers to that school's first NCAA title in volleyball in 1995, and 13 years later authored, *Talent and the Secret Life of Teams*, a collection of essays, columns, and creative writing on leadership and team building.

He certainly informed the pledge I make today to my mentees as well as my clients for my therapy practice, Jeannie Lynch, LPC-S, NCC, LLC: "I will never ask you to go somewhere that I am not willing to go myself." There is an integrity, a transparency, that you need to have in both situations that is integral to both relationships.

In a therapeutic relationship, I have to keep very clear boundaries. There's not a lot of personal disclosure from me during therapy. When I'm in a mentor/mentee relationship, however, I really pour into people on a more personal level. I'm more likely to share insights from specific past experiences, some of which were traumatic. I model authenticity and describe situations I have come through in my own life: the struggle, the application, and the victory on the other side. Therefore, I don't choose to mentor just anybody. I mentor those who are really motivated and are going to benefit greatly from my mentoring. After all, if I am going to put 110 percent into a person, I need that person to put 110 percent in as well. I will work as hard as they do, but I will not work harder than they do because that is called "enabling." It is all about mentoring those who really want to get it. That's what gives me the most satisfaction and gives the mentee the most value.

From 1998 to 2016, I mentored a young woman who came

into our relationship knowing nothing about addiction counseling. She followed me to all the places I was employed during that time. She got her bachelor's and master's degrees, and then sat under me for clinical supervision for two years to get her professional counseling (LPC) license. She was teachable and wanted to be a good therapist. I had the tools to teach her, showing her everything I knew. The most significant things I taught her were how to have authenticity and to meet the client where they are. The greatest asset you can bring into a counseling relationship is yourself. Being able to listen actively, being direct and honest, and going straight to the pain of the individual is the foundation of therapy.

Today, she is extremely successful in the field. She is clinical director of a three-county mental health system. True success as a mentor is seeing your mentee achieve what they set out to do, and she certainly did.

As a mentor, my secret to success comes from my passion to grow people. My gift is to meet them where they are and use wisdom to discern their potential. I also understand when to push, when to nurture, and when to encourage, having a sixth sense to know what is needed for them in any given situation. One of my most rewarding experiences as a mentor was when I worked with Jessica. I met her in June 2014. She was 27 at that time and newly married. I was serving alongside her husband at our church. I'd later learn that at first Jessica was extremely jealous of me. She said I looked like I had it all together, and I was attractive, even if I was in my late fifties at that time. Her jealousy stemmed from the fact that Jessica didn't trust

The Best Version

women at all. She started attending one of the small study groups I ran at the church, and I could tell she wanted to leave that very first day. I also knew she was there for a purpose.

I took her under my wing, and the rest is history. Jessica had been involved in a very traumatic car accident when she was 19 years old. She sustained brain damage and should have died. She did have some cognitive deficits from the brain damage, and all of her life others had told her she was "stupid." That made her buy into the lie that she couldn't do anything. I discovered that Jessica really wanted to help people, and I nurtured that in our mentoring.

It wasn't easy. In fact, we had to take a break for about a year because Jessica wasn't progressing forward. At times, situational depression paralyzed her. But going through that struggle helped Jessica come into a new place where she started seeing what she needed to do differently. Slowly but surely, she began to trust, first me, and then other women. Through that, Jessica began to trust herself and to truly see the potential and gifts she had inside of her: childlike innocence, purity of heart, and love for others, particularly women, to help them through their challenges. Jessica even discovered that she could be a leader.

She has been involved in my small groups at church ever since, and in 2019, by the grace of God, she started her own small study group of women. Jessica is doing a phenomenal job. She has a full group of women of all different ages, and she challenges them, loves them, and nurtures them. She is also happily married and raising a beautiful two-year-old daughter. There is no finer reward for me than to see Jessica believing in herself.

As a mentee, I believe I'm good at receiving mentoring because I'm hungry. I want to learn. I am a seeker, and I am not afraid of doing the hard work to continue becoming the best version of myself. In December 2015, I applied and was accepted into a leadership program called Epic Church Leadership Institute (ECLI). It takes 20 applicants a year for a 15-month program, and it is designed to help those who want to go into ministry work be able to push themselves spiritually, physically, and emotionally. It is very intense, utilizing such things as physical workouts and time management training. I was 57 going on 58 at that time and the oldest person in the group, but being a former athlete, I was up for a challenge. It may not have been pretty at times, but I didn't quit. I pushed through, and I found out I was capable of doing much more than I ever thought. ECLI helped me be a much more rounded mentor and leader, and the relationships that came out of that have been priceless to me. One of those, Dr. Jana Lovelace, has become like a sister to me and a partner in ministry. Together, we co-founded No Limits Women's Conferences, LLC, an organization that exists to bridge the gap between life's struggles for women and spirituality.

I have a lot of passion and intensity which are sometimes misinterpreted by people. My emotional nature can cause me to have knee jerk reactions from time to time that I am working to improve. I am a clinical supervisor for people who have graduated from master's programs and who are working towards their licenses as counselors. I have many requests for clinical supervision, and there is a tremendous liability that goes along with accepting those requests. I become responsible for the work they do. My licensing is on the line, so I am very particular about the folks I take on. We must be a match ethically and with our values. I could take up to four at a time,

The Best Version

but I only take two. They come to me because they know my intensity and passion about counseling. The same is true with spiritual mentees. They want to be mentored by me because they know how I feel about people growing and maturing.

How do I know when I have achieved my goal as a mentor? It's usually by my mentee's actions. If I am a good mentor, I'm going to see their progress—and it is not my accomplishment being manifested. It is their achievement.

I challenge everyone to do two things. First, find someone a little more inexperienced than you are in your field, your businesses, your relationships, or your life, and mentor them to become the best version of themselves. Second, find someone who is above where you are in any of those areas and be mentored by them, for it is then that you can become the best version of yourself.

Jeannie Lynch has a passion for connecting with people and seeing them improve the quality of their life. She has a private practice in Decatur, Alabama where she works with dual diagnosis, addiction/mental illness, codependency, grief, trauma abuse, stress management, relationship issues, and other behavioral disorders. She also offers consultation services and is an author and motivational speaker with a whole focus of guiding women to freedom. Contact Jeannie at jlynchlpc@gmail.com.

NOTES

1 Robert G. C. Waite, *The Psychopathic God: Adolph Hitler* (New York: Basic Books, 1977) 244-45.

16

Trust and Confidence

Vernette Elliott

AS I HELP and mentor others, I stick to a tried-and-true motto based on the words of Luke 6:31 from the Bible. "Do unto others as you would have them do unto you." Then I add: "Even if you don't like them."
That's not surprising. After all, mentoring is not about me. It is all about helping somebody else, and if I was going to identify my first guiding force, One who still propels me today, it is God. He certainly set the standard for caring about people, including those who aren't especially likable—a principle I've learned to apply throughout my mentoring experiences as I established trust and confidence within myself and others.

My faith-focused background came from my upbringing. I was born in 1952 in the heart of the south, the state of Alabama, and deep into segregation in America. But social issues and civil rights weren't what I was thinking about when I was a little girl. The ninth and last child of my mother, Eunice, and father, Leroy, I'm careful to tell people that I'm the youngest, but I am not the baby of my family. I never felt that way and was never treated that way. I did not require a lot of coddling. I was introverted, though, often lost in playful imagination and largely unaware of the racial divisiveness of the times, though that would certainly impact me later on.

My parents were good parents. They were strong in their faith, and church was very important to our family. We went to church every weekend, including Sunday School before the regular service and Baptist Training Union in the evening. We participated in Friday youth group, choir practices, and other church events such as revivals and conferences. My mom and dad said Sunday was set aside for the Lord. That was the rule of the house, and there were no exceptions.

Since I came along when my parents were in their forties, most of my eight brothers and sisters were already adults and the rest were about to leave home, leaving me to be raised with my sister, Eulylia, and my nephew, Anthony. My sister, Annie Ruth, was already married and became like a second mother to me. She and her husband, Maurice, were such a big influence in my life. Annie Ruth had very high standards, and they made sure that I participated in the college preparation program in high school and reviewed my report card along with my parents. I went to summer school because they thought there were classes I needed to take to be better prepared for life after high school. Annie Ruth was one of my role models.

My mom did not have a career. Whenever she faced a difficult task, she always said it was not going to beat her. This taught me tenacity and strength. She learned how to be a good seamstress, upholster furniture, wallpaper walls, make canned fruits and vegetables, and make a dollar go a long way. My mother also took care of my dad's mother until she died, and I never once heard her complain. My daddy worked at the Decatur Oil

Mill. He was there for many years until they closed, and then he worked for a moving company until he retired. My parents taught us so much about family. They loved each one of us and never played the favorite game. They had large expectations of us. To this day, family means a lot to me and my siblings. People tell us that we take care of each other, and it is true.

In addition, if mom and dad could help someone in the community, they did it without a lot of fanfare. If anyone was hungry and needed a meal, my parents welcomed them into our home. It used to be called Eunice's Café. On Sunday after church it was never just our family at the house. When we went to the baseball and football games in the community, my parents' station wagon would be filled with kids. I don't know how we all got in there or what we did, but they were always at our house. It was a lot of love, a lot of giving. I saw the life they lived, and they never wanted for anything because God always provided for them.

It's no wonder, then, that our family never knew any lack. In fact, I didn't realize I came from a low-income home until I got to college and studied economics. My parents never talked about what we were financially. They wanted us to be what we could be. They never once told me that I couldn't have or do something. Instead, they prayed, and God always showed them what to do. That's just how it was.

———

The racial divide in America really didn't hit me until after I started junior high school. I saw the different marches and protests on the news, but the incident that had the biggest impact on me was the Sunday morning bombing of the 16th Street Baptist Church in Birmingham, Alabama on September 15, 1963 that took the lives of four young girls. I was 11, and I didn't fully understand it because the adults didn't talk about it in front of the kids. But I recall getting ready to go to church and being somewhat frightened, wondering if somebody was going to bomb us. I remember asking, "Mom, do you mean to tell me those were little girls my age that got killed?" After that, my awareness of the civil rights movement began to grow as I tried to focus on my education.

Education was important to my parents. I never thought I couldn't go to college because of lack of funds or anything like that—and, as it turned out, my sister, Eulylia, and I did just that, as did my nephew, Anthony. He studied urban planning at Alabama A&M University, one of the Historically Black Colleges and Universities, and my sister went to the same school and majored in home economics with a minor in early childhood education. I thought about going to Auburn University, a predominantly white school, because of their home economics program, but after attending Austin High School and being in a predominantly white atmosphere there with no help, no recognition of my achievements, and no encouragement because of my race, I applied to Alabama A&M. The racial divisiveness of the times had indeed impacted me, but I thoroughly enjoyed it there, pursuing a degree in bachelor's degree in home economics and a minor in early childhood education.

My senior year in college, I was recruited by the federal government and offered an internship for three years in the career field of procurement. I accepted the opportunity with the approval of my husband, Anthony. His support was vital because it mandated a move to St. Louis, MO, and a change in career for him. I never envisioned myself moving from Alabama and being away from my family. I got married at the age of 20, and we had a baby the following year. Our daughter was ill for the first five years of her life, and it was a stressful time. I constantly called my parents for guidance and prayers, and they often came to visit us.

It was during that trying time that I first realized it was not all about me. I had to think about the impact of my decisions on two other people, my husband and daughter. My parents helped me understand there were two sides to every story and that I should always consider my family. Today, when I mentor others, I remember the lessons I learned back then and teach that there is always more than one approach to a situation that must be considered when working with others. We cannot be so demanding that our way is the only way.

I have had the privilege as a mentor to see people develop and get promoted. Several came into the government as interns, just as I did, and were eventually promoted into supervisory positions. I believe mentoring can be formal, informal, or situational. I have used all three over the years, and each type of mentoring uses different styles and approaches. I met with mentees or staff members on a weekly basis, and I set goals for procurement processes with clear strategies and milestones for accomplishing each action. I kept an effective development plan that ensured each mentee maintained their proficiency and sustained open and regular communications with them. I believe the success in mentoring comes from the synergy it creates and the trust and confidence it produces. It's not that the two of you will agree on everything, but it's that you're understanding one another and working together. What result is the mentee looking for? What are you looking for in working with that person? I love contributing to a person's success and seeing them grow and mature.

Early in my career at the Aviation Research and Development Command that was later merged into the Aviation Systems Command, Donna was transitioning out of administration into procurement. My supervisor thought I'd be a good mentor for her, but she and I bumped heads all the time. We worked together well enough, but there was always a pull. One day Donna was very honest. She said she didn't really care for me a whole lot. I told her I felt likewise—but I added that if we stuck to our mentoring relationship, she'd know what she was doing and why she was doing it. She wouldn't be floundering. We carried on, and with lots of prayer, Donna and I began to understand each other. Ultimately, we really became very good friends. Today, over 30 years later, we still are. When we're together she'll tell others, "This is the lady that trained me and taught me what I know." She even invited me to her husband's funeral service.

On another occasion, I had the opportunity to mentor a young man named Dwight. He was an intern recently hired by the Aviation Systems Command, and as we worked together, he sometimes had to redo assignments. However, we built a rapport, and when I was assigned as a contracting officer for a major Should Cost Team in the organization, I chose Dwight as one of my contract specialists. Years later, I saw Dwight again, and he introduced me as the person who taught him everything he knows about procurement. It was humbling and an honor to hear him say that.

I try to use all my past mentoring experiences as building blocks. Some of my steppingstones were there to help other people know what to look out for, go forward, and not be afraid. When I was in St. Louis working as an intern with the

Trust and Confidence

Aviation Systems Command, I was in a role where I didn't have very much to do. Frustrated, I went to my supervisor, but he continued to assign me mundane tasks. He was an ex-Marine, and he had a reputation for kind of being a bully. "This is not me," I told him. "I don't just sit on a job. You've got to give me something to do."

In response, he gave me an assignment with the AH-1 helicopter and told me to "sink or swim." I did not have a mentor, but the attitude I'd seen in my mother rose up within me, and I decided I was not going to let the situation beat me. I prayed, and I was guided to the right person to ask questions and get answers. I made mistakes, but I learned lessons that I used for future acquisitions. I got some bruises but did not sink, and I earned the respect of my immediate supervisor. I also learned that I would never treat someone the same way. Every person who worked for me had a trainer, and my door was always open to discuss any issues they had.

Perhaps my biggest challenge as a mentor came when I had been working nine years with the Target Acquisition Designation Sight/Pilot Night Vision Sensor with Martin Marietta (now Lockheed Martin). I was kind of worn out because it was a part of another major program and required a lot of travel, but I was grieving, too, because my father had just passed away. I went to my supervisor and asked him for a change. He didn't want to do it because it would require more from him, and it was a disruption no one wanted. When he finally relented and met my request, he put me in charge of 15 workers in a section that had a challenging mixture of procurement requirements. I quickly discovered I had been thrust into a hostile environment. When I first arrived, they all gathered around me like a pack of wolves.

"What are you going to do for us?" one lady asked. She was rude and got right up in my face. I inched forward so we were toe-to-toe. "Everybody is looking at you, even the people from the other shop, but I am not going to allow you all up in my face. You are going to have to step back. Then I will talk to you." Then I addressed the entire group. "You *all* will move back, and I will talk to you individually as your section chief and work with you."

I saw a lot of eye rolling and wondered, *What in the world have I walked into?*

As the days progressed, I found out. The workers all had low self-esteem because they felt like nobody cared about them. Their workload was tremendous, and there were certain procurements that were over a year-and-a-half old that they had not been able to get out. When I started looking at the history of the section, I couldn't understand how the situation had been allowed to get that bad. Harold Mabrey, a person I looked up to as a mentor, always told me, "Never go in assuming anything. Do your research and find out."

So, I did, and I learned that no one had taken the time to train the workers properly. They were called misfits, and they felt that way. I went to the appropriate office and formed an integrated project team. I told my staff I was going to work with them to correct the mistakes that had been made. Within a year, we had reformed that office and developed very positive relationships. Hostility was replaced with respect. Trust and confidence were established. They went on to get awards and recognition—and one of the best things that ever happened to me in my career was when they gave me a surprise party for Boss's Day.

No one had taken the time to love on them until I arrived—and that's how I found out that people really don't always care about how much you know. It's about how much you care.

No man is an island. Everyone needs guidance and help. Why go down a bumpy road by yourself making a lot of mistakes when you can have the experience, knowledge, and skills of another individual and benefit from that person's professional or personal development? Receiving mentoring is an experience that you can never put a price on, and it can be used to enhance your learning and development in all walks of life. Being a mentor is not always easy, but it is a joy when you watch someone succeed, achieve results, and reap the benefits from the trust and confidence established between yourself and the mentee.

Vernette Elliott has served for 35 years as a contract specialist, supervisory contract specialist, division director, and director for multiple federal agencies procuring major weapons systems, support services, and information technology. During this time, Vernette developed into a career procurement professional and a willing mentor, focused on providing her staff with the right skills to assume the right jobs to achieve balanced and productive working relationships. Contact Vernette at davinanicole@outlook.com